# DEDICATION

I want to dedicate this book and the entire **At Your Best** Playbook series to my parents: Dolores and Giovanni (Juan) for their courage, hard work and perseverance in the pursuit of our family's American Dream. For me, it has always been about "family first" and I've been blessed with a great son, Adam, of whom I cannot be prouder. I am so grateful to have my sisters' and brothers' support—one of whom, my brother Hector, I particularly want to thank for being so instrumental in helping me turn this AYB Playbook into reality. Finally, I want to thank my beautiful wife, Ginny, for being my one and only; for inspiring me throughout this **At Your Best** journey; and for all our wonderful years together. I look forward to the rest of our American Dream.

# DEDICATION

# CONTENTS

## PART 2: At Your Best as an HVAC/R Technician: Becoming a World-Class Player

## PART 3: At Your Best as a Small Business: Building a World-Class Franchise

# PREFACE

## THE AMERICAN DREAM IS ALIVE AND WELL

My parents brought our family to the United States from Argentina in 1963 in search of the American Dream. With hard work and perseverance, my parents provided my four sisters, my two brothers and me the building blocks on which to pursue and realize our own dreams. The most remarkable thing about my family's American Dream story is how unremarkable and commonplace our story really is. Tens of millions of examples of our story exist among native-born and immigrant Americans—past and present—who rose beyond their original circumstances to build a fruitful life for themselves and their families.

There is no other country on Earth—other than the United States of America—where an individual or family can start with nothing and expect solid, good odds that they will realize their own version of the American Dream—as long as they work hard, get an education, learn the skills that are in demand and persevere in their pursuits.

The definition of "American Dream" can mean many things to people but it usually comes down to:

✓ Personal Freedom
✓ Opportunity of Choices
✓ Building a Better Future for Yourself and Your Family
✓ Achieving Your Goals and Dreams

I truly believe that the American Dream is still very much alive and going strong. However, I also believe that most people may not know how to put together a plan and then execute it to get themselves on the path to fulfilling their own American Dream. They also may not know that the Skilled Trades offer a wide array of tremendous opportunities. One of the tried and true paths to attaining one's Dream is by pursuing a career in one of the Skilled Trades, as my father did.

I am convinced that if given a realistic plan that clearly lays out what it takes to build a successful career in one of the Skilled Trades, along with how to build a successful small business in that trade, people will act. With such a plan, an individual will have a starting point, along with a breakdown of additional resources and the milestones to shoot for to get from Point A to Point B, and so on until they reach their goal. That is why I wrote this and the other books in the **At Your Best** Playbook series and launched the www.AtYourBest.com website.

I absolutely believe that you are **At Your Best** when you have a game plan. Let **At Your Best** be the foundation for your own personal plan, your starting point and your path to *your* American Dream.

# INTRODUCTION

## THE SKILLED TRADES AND THE AMERICAN DREAM

Today, there are over **6.5 million** unfilled yet well-paying and fulfilling positions in the United States in the Skilled Trades. These positions remain unfilled—not because there aren't enough people available and interested in having a secure, well-paying job, but because there are not enough people with the skills, attitude and experience required for these positions. This is what is called The Skills Gap: the difference between the available jobs requiring specific skills and the available people with those skills to do those jobs.

Over the last decades, a misguided view has taken hold in our society that minimizes the importance and opportunity represented by careers in the Skilled Trades. Despite reality, a career in the Skilled Trades has come to be seen as a sort of "consolation prize" as compared to a career of sitting behind a desk with a four-year college degree. The time has never been more right to do away with this shortsighted, highly detrimental perspective and get back to appreciating the fact that the Skilled Trades are the foundational building blocks of our country's quality of life.

The Skills Gap is at its widest ever and, unfortunately, it is expected to continue widening in the future. Be assured that we will all feel the growing impact of this Skills Gap. However, for you, this is an enormous and potentially life-changing opportunity. Whether the US economy is growing or stalling or contracting, your personal economic picture will always be better, relatively speaking, as long as you have a set of skills and experience that are in demand in your local marketplace and throughout the country.

The Skills Gap is real. The lack of good people building long-term, fulfilling and well-paying careers is real. In a matter of a few months during 2017–2018, the US economy went from a state of high unemployment levels to one that public officials and the media call "full employment" levels. Still, there remain tens of millions of people who are unemployed or underemployed, while The Skills Gap continues to widen. Those still on the sidelines or in jobs that do not utilize their potential have an opportunity that is real. The opportunity for you to future-proof your life and that of your family's by entering the Skilled Trades is real. The opportunity for you to earn a secure, comfortable, middle-class income for the rest of your career is very real.

The objective of this **At Your Best** (AYB) Playbook is to provide you with a high-level, play-by-play approach to enable you to take advantage of what that Skills Gap can mean to you—a path to securing one of those well-paying and rewarding positions in the Skilled Trades. This AYB Playbook is intended to provide you the most comprehensive resource available to help you through each step of building your career and launching a small business as an HVAC/R Technician. Throughout it, you will be directed to other important resources that can provide you immediately actionable information to learn even more about a critical topic. My hope is that this AYB Playbook will become your plan of action for building and securing your American Dream so that you can be **At Your Best**.

## "KITCHEN TABLE" MOMENTS & AT YOUR BEST

Think of a **"Kitchen Table Moment"** as a time-out session that you take to think through and lay out your next set of plays or to rethink some portion of your game plan. You are reading this book because you or someone important to you is considering a job or a career in one of the Skilled Trades. You may be sitting at your kitchen table, alone or with someone important to you, trying to think through what the right steps are to take to ensure that you will be successful. Unless you have a family member or friend, who has "been there, done that," to coach you and open doors, you are on your own during this and your future kitchen table moments.

The AYB Playbook series is intended to change that. Each Playbook is designed to first lay out a high-level, play-by-play approach to walk you through stages of building a successful career in one of the Skilled Trades. It is written to address both the needs and circumstances of someone who is starting to consider entering the Skilled Trades as well as someone who is looking to get their career on a more solid, positive track. Then, AYB Playbooks present a process for launching and building a successful, small business in the Skilled Trades.

Obviously, every Kitchen Table Moment will vary for each person and their specific circumstances. However, no matter who you are and what your circumstances may be along the way, you will have questions about what to do next and whether it makes sense for you to take that step. AYB Playbooks are designed to help guide you through these Kitchen Table Moments so that you can consider the right questions and issues AND you can hold yourself accountable to maximize your opportunity for success.

## AT YOUR BEST AS AN HVAC/R TECHNICIAN

A successful career in the Skilled Trades is a tried and true, proven platform from which to launch a successful and lucrative small business. A career as an HVAC/R (Heating, Ventilation, Air Conditioning and

Refrigeration) Technician is one of the most versatile of the Skilled Trades, giving you the skills, hands-on experience and understanding of how buildings and other structures are built to meet our needs and provide us all with the quality of life we enjoy.

As long as society needs homes, offices and all other types of building to be heated, ventilated, and cooled, there will be a demand for HVAC technicians. As long as we need our foods, medicines and items and substances of all types to be refrigerated, there will be jobs for skilled refrigeration technicians. As long as these HVAC/R systems need to be installed, maintained, modified or repaired, a skilled HVAC/R tech will always be able to find work.

**Please note:** Given that the skills and experience needed to succeed as an HVAC technician are nearly identical to those needed by a refrigeration technician, we will use the term "HVAC/R technician" to discuss both specialties.

This AYB Playbook presents what it takes to build a great career as an HVAC/R Technician and how to use that experience to launch a successful and lucrative small business. This AYB Playbook will work to answer the following questions:

1. What does a career as an HVAC/R Technician look like?
2. Why should you consider becoming an HVAC/R Technician?
3. How do you become a successful Craftsman as an HVAC/R Technician?
4. How much can you make as an HVAC/R Technician?
5. What are your career options once you become an HVAC/R Technician?
6. How long does it take to be successful at each stage in an HVAC/R Technician's career?
7. How and where do you find work as an HVAC/R Technician?

8. What are the specific, concrete actions you can take to become a highly valued employee?

9. What does it take to strike out on your own? And

10. What—at minimum—does it take to launch and build a successful small business?

Before we get into answering these questions, we need to cover some foundational concepts about being **At Your Best**. This AYB Playbook is divided into three parts:

✓ **Part 1** presents the **At Your Best** fundamentals—rules of the game—that will be at play throughout this AYB Playbook

✓ **Part 2** provides you a game plan with the steps, process and some concrete actions to take consistently in order to build a successful career as an HVAC/R Technician

✓ **Part 3** provides you a game plan for launching and building a successful small business as an HVAC/R Technician

# ABOUT THE AUTHOR

On the face of it, you might ask yourself, "What does a guy with an MBA from University of Michigan in finance and marketing, who spent nearly thirty years helping technology startups and turnarounds drive the sales, business development and marketing efforts, know about the Skilled Trades?" Well, I also manage our family real estate investment business and have renovated multiple properties in Seattle, New York City, St. Louis, Atlanta, Kansas and Michigan, which afforded me the opportunity to get to know and work with many skilled tradespeople and contractors across the US.

The inspiration for this **At Your Best** Playbook series came in part from the many discussions I had with these small business owners. Irrespective of where in the US, they all spoke of the lack of qualified tradespeople that limited their ability to grow their businesses. The thing is that, as I started to grasp the real-world, detrimental consequences of what this nationwide shortage really means to all of us, it became a kind of mission for me to talk to anyone even remotely connected to any of the Skilled Trades. Once I started to factor in the very real, human impact that reversing this situation could have on individuals and their families—folks like veterans and people who are unemployed or under-employed—**At Your Best** became my 24/7 passion.

# PART 1:

# At Your Best Fundamentals: The Rules of the Game

As you read this AYB Playbook, you will want to keep a number of foundational concepts in mind to provide context for what we will be discussing. Part 1 specifically lays out the AYB Fundamentals, so you can refer to them as you progress through this AYB Playbook.

This section will describe:

- ✓ How this AYB Playbook and the www.AtYourBest.com website together are designed to provide you the action plan and tools to be successful at each stage in your career and in your small business
  - • The sources and methods used to create the content you will find in this AYB Playbook
- ✓ Who the AYB Playbook series was created to help and how they can use AYB Playbooks to build a successful career and launch a thriving small business
- ✓ Some basic truths about taking on an **At Your Best** mindset
  - • It all begins with You, Inc.
  - • 3P+A = People, Performance, Professionalism and Attitude

# CHAPTER 1

# AYB Playbooks & www.AtYourBest.com

# YOU ARE AT YOUR BEST
## *when you have the right tools for the job.*

---

## AYB PLAYBOOKS & WWW.ATYOURBEST.COM

AYB Playbooks and the **At Your Best** website are designed to work together to give you access to the broadest set of resources you may need as you build your career and business. The AYB Playbooks are kept short and concise to make them easy to read and keep close by for easy, quick reference. The www.AtYourBest.com site is designed to include all the additional resources and tools to help you become successful.

AYB Playbooks are intended to present you with a clear, direct path to reach key stages in a career in a specific Skilled Trade. The path is laid out as a set of milestones and checklists that you can use to hold yourself accountable, like a game plan. However, AYB Playbooks are specifically designed to be concise versus all-encompassing. You will be given easy-to-use starting points so that you can move to the next to-do or milestone.

Bottom line: This AYB Playbook is intended to provide you a pathway to follow, with the important waypoints along the way, to a successful career in the Skilled Trades. This AYB Playbook will present:

✓ What to consider when thinking about starting your career in the Skilled Trades

3

✓ How and where to get the training you need to start your career

✓ What steps you need to take to build a successful career

✓ How to capitalize on the skills and experience you build during your career to launch a successful small business

✓ Which critical success factors you need to focus on to maximize your potential for success as a small business in the Skilled Trades

The various career and business planning tools and worksheets described in this AYB Playbook are available on our website in the **AYB Quick Tools** section. The inventory of **AYB Quick Tools** will grow well beyond those described in the AYB Playbook, as readers and website visitors request additional tools. So, please visit our website regularly. If you cannot find what you need or would like, let us know and we will try to create it and make it available for everyone.

"A look beyond the horizon" is how one of the AYB Subject Matter Experts described what he wished that he could have had while he was building his career and his very successful general contracting business. That is what I hope to offer you with the AYB Playbooks and our www.AtYourBest.com website—to give you a view of what you will likely need or encounter if you pursue a particular course of action, so you can a make better decision before you get there.

The content in AYB Playbooks is supplemented with additional content and resources and access to the AYB community of other readers and subject matter experts via the AYB website. The objective is that as more readers visit our website and provide their comments, questions and interests, the site will continually improve to serve our readers.

*"Subject Matter Expert?"—Not really. I am just a guy who loved what I did: building homes to the best of my ability with a great team of craftsmen who stuck with me because I stuck with them. Our customers kept coming back because we were always fair and honest with the good and the ugly.*

—JEFF M., RETIRED CONTRACTOR, ST. LOUIS

## AT YOUR BEST WITH SUBJECT MATTER EXPERTS

The content in AYB Playbooks will provide you insights from an array of real-world, Subject Matter Experts (SME). Each SME was selected because of their success in their respective expertise.

SMEs were consulted at each stage of developing the **At Your Best** Playbook series. Collectively, their role, as presented through their quotes and words of wisdom, is to provide you a "look beyond the horizon." As they say, "to be forewarned is to be forearmed." The objective of AYB Playbooks is to help to minimize the unknowns ahead as you consider a career in the skilled trades.

To a person, SMEs stress that there is no shortcut or work-around for the time, good attitude, hard work and perseverance needed to acquire the education, skills and experience to become successful as a Craftsman in the skilled trades. Every SME is just as adamant that if you are prepared to put in the time and do the hard work to become a true Craftsman, you will find yourself with little competition and much success in your choice of jobs in your chosen Skilled Trade.

Good Attitude    Education
Hard Work    +    Skills    =    Success
Perseverance    Experience

To review a few of the SME interviews conducted for developing the AYB Playbook series, go to www.AtYourBest.com and click on "**AYB Quick Tools.**" You will find a link to "**Getting Your Head Straight.**" The comments provided by the SMEs are presented under: "SME Insights." Highlights of each SME interview is presented in bullet form for easy reference with a link to a longer, downloadable version with the rest of the SME insights. SMEs have "been there, done that" and each of them happily volunteered their views hoping to help you on your journey to become a Craftsman.

## SOURCES, METHODS AND CREDIBILITY

An overriding objective of the AYB Playbook series and our website—www.AtYourBest.com—is to present you with a logical and easy-to-follow plan of action drawn from current, credible sources.

A wide variety of sources were used to create the AYB Playbooks and AYB website. The content associated with Part 2 of this AYB Playbook, which relates to building your career, was drawn from the following sources:

✓ Interviews with Subject Matter Experts
  • Successful players in the Skilled Trades—current & retired
✓ *Occupational Outlook Handbook, 2016–2017*, US Dept. of Labor
✓ www.CareerOneStop.org, US Dept. of Labor
✓ O*NET Online, US Dept. of Labor
✓ WOIS Career Information System
  • A nonprofit organization dedicated to compiling and publishing career data

Also, toward the end of Part 2, Chapter 7 presents several important, concrete actions that you can take consistently throughout your career to become a highly valued employee in every position you will hold in the future. I will be recommending that you continue learning more about these "concrete actions" by directing you to specific sections in an excellent book called:

✓ *How to Be the Employee Your Company Can't Live Without: 18 Ways to Become Indispensable* by Glenn Shepard

The content presented in Part 3—covering launching and building your small business—was largely developed in response to the guidance and key issues raised during my interviews with AYB's Subject Matter Experts. At a high level, this section covers a number of critical topics.

These critical topics areas include:
✓ What to consider when starting a small business
✓ What you must do to operate a successful small business
✓ High impact, low cost marketing strategies to attract customers
✓ Competitive advantage through excellent customer service
✓ Leadership and management of small teams

To provide a comprehensive treatment of these critical topics, while keeping the length of this AYB Playbook to something reasonable, I chose several books to help provide you what you need to know. Although there are an almost unlimited number of books and resources out there that do a great job of addressing each of the topics above, I chose and referenced one book for each of the critical topics. In my opinion, each of these authors speak directly to what it takes to be **At Your Best**.

The books I selected are:

- ✓ *Small Time Operator*, 13th edition by Bernard Kamoroff
- ✓ *The Art of the Start* by Guy Kawasaki
- ✓ *Guerrilla Marketing Remix*, by Jay Conrad Levison & Jeannie Levinson
- ✓ *Raving Fans: A Revolutionary Approach to Customer Service* by Ken Blanchard & Sheldon Bowles
- ✓ *Extreme Ownership: How U.S. Navy SEALs Lead and Win* by Jocko Willink & Leif Babin

Whenever we discuss a critical topic that draws on the books noted above, I will provide you an easy-to-use approach to finding further important information on that particular subject through the use of an **AYB Assist** which we will explain later. For now, an **AYB Assist** will give you the specific location in one or more of these books where you can go and learn more about a specific subject. Please note that I strongly encourage you to purchase your own copies of these six excellent books to use to gain a greater understanding of critical concepts presented in this AYB Playbook.

## LOCAL AND ACTIONABLE

**At Your Best** is committed to providing you with the information that you will need to make decisions during your Kitchen Table Moments. Just as importantly, the information that you find in AYB Playbooks will be immediately actionable and available in your local community. In other words, no matter where you live or want to live in the US, AYB Playbooks can help you walk through each next step of your career in the Skilled Trades.

## ———— CHAPTER 1 REPLAY ————
## AYB Playbooks & www.AtYourBest.com

» AYB Playbooks and the AYB website provide you a pathway for launching a successful career and small business in the Skilled Trades by laying out the critical success factors for you to consider and the steps to follow to achieve success

» AYB Playbooks and website provide actionable information that is immediately usable wherever you may live in the US, drawing on the insights of key reference sources, numerous Subject Matter Experts who have "been there, done that," and six great books

# CHAPTER 2

# AYB Playbooks
# Are for You, If . . .

# YOU ARE AT YOUR BEST
## *when you know you are on the right path.*

---

*I can say the willingness to get dirty has always defined us as a nation, and it's a hallmark of hard work and a hallmark of fun, and dirt is not the enemy.*

—MIKE ROWE,
TV PERSONALITY AND SKILLED TRADES ADVOCATE

---

## WHO THIS AYB PLAYBOOK IS FOR . . .

All over this country, there are millions of people who are unemployed for whatever reason. Many others are underemployed doing a job that is not what they want or that pays them less than what they need. A large majority of these folks are prepared to put in the work and effort to learn the skills to secure their future. So many would gladly pursue a new career in the Skilled Trades. However, due to many reasons, they just don't know how to take the first step(s), and then the next and so on.

**At Your Best** Playbooks are intended for:

✓ The Newcomers—Those who are entering the workforce for the first time

✓ The Veterans—Those who are entering the civilian workforce after military service

✓ The Restarters—Those who are looking to change or reestablish career paths

✓ The Upgraders—Those who are already in a Skilled Trade but want to take their career to the next level or who are entrepreneurs in that Skilled Trade wanting to drive their businesses to greater heights

## *The Newcomers*

Anyone entering the workforce for the first time should consider the Skilled Trades as a viable and potentially lucrative career. Whether you are about to graduate from high school, or college, or a person in an unskilled, minimum wage, "dead-end" job, one of the Skilled Trades could offer you a great career. Take a moment to imagine entering a career that, right from the start, pays you a reliable, living wage, where your income increases in direct relationship to the experience and skills that you acquire. Imagine earning a solid, middle-class income in the time it takes to attend a four-year university—without all the college debt!

AYB Playbooks are intended to help you consider whether a career in one of the Skilled Trades is *right* for you. Each AYB Playbook walks you through a logical process so that you can understand what it takes to be successful and how to get there in a particular Skilled Trade. Just as importantly, each AYB Playbook is designed as a minimum set of steps and milestones you will need to take to realize that success.

**If you are a Newcomer:** Use this AYB Playbook to help guide yourself through the important decisions and the key milestones that you will face during your career in the Skilled Trades.

## The Veterans

Military Veterans are among this country's most valuable human assets. If you are a vet, the experience and maturity you gained as a member of the US Armed Forces make you a tremendous, and sometimes untapped, resource for our economy. Given what you have done for our country, the rest of us simply cannot do enough to repay your contribution and sacrifice to protect our way of life. AYB Playbooks are intended to help you and other Veterans hit the ground running with an actionable plan on how to build a successful career in the Skilled Trades.

**If you are a Veteran:** Use this AYB Playbook to help you transition to a successful career as a civilian. Your past training and experience will allow you to jump forward into a new career and this Playbook will point out additional resources available to you.

## The Restarters

Every day, it seems, we read or watch stories of folks who have been let go from a job that they have been doing for years with a company that either reduced its workforce through automation, sent its manufacturing overseas, or went out of business altogether. With all the economic turmoil of the recent past, so many of our fellow citizens are currently either unemployed (looking for a new job/career) or underemployed (working jobs that pay much less and that hardly draws on their accumulated skills and abilities). Throughout our country, we also have folks who have made mistakes in their past and are now looking to regain their footing in society by building new futures that can make meaningful contributions to their communities and families. AYB Playbooks are designed to help Restarters jump-start your pursuit of a new career in the Skilled Trades.

**If you are a Restarter:** Use this Playbook to help you transition into your new career by showing you where you can jump in depending your past training and experience.

## The Upgraders

Even if you are currently working in the Skilled Trades, you may have been stuck in a role that limits your aspirations for whatever reason. Sometimes, when you are too focused on doing the job at hand and earning a paycheck so you can pay the bills, it seems like you don't have time to come up for air. This can happen to any of us, even though we may know better and we know that we should be planning for the future. It may be that you have the skills and knowledge to take on more and move up, but you don't know what your next steps should be. AYB Playbooks are designed so that anyone currently working in the Skilled Trades can jump right in, so you can fine tune or upgrade your career path.

**If you are an Upgrader:** Use this Playbook to "see beyond" the day-to-day of doing the job so that you can consider what career options are available to you and what you may need to do to backfill a missed step or skills and what steps to take to start being your own boss. If you're already an entrepreneur and running your business, use this Playbook to help guide your team members as they build their career and use it to consider additional steps that can help you drive your business to new heights.

*There are no such things as coulda, shoulda, or woulda. If you coulda and shoulda, you woulda done it.*

—PAT RILEY

## AYB Playbooks Are for You, If . . .

AYB Playbooks are designed for those people who are the *exact opposite* of the "shoulda, woulda, coulda" kind of people. If you are a person who just won't quit when something you want to do and working for get tough, the Skilled Trades and this AYB Playbook are for you. If you are a person who can commit to a completing a project—large or small— with an eye for doing high quality work, the Skilled Trades and this AYB Playbook are for you. If you are a person who wants to take charge of your life and, with a lot of hard work and perseverance, learn a set of skills that will be in demand for the rest of your life, the Skilled Trades and this AYB Playbook are for you. If this doesn't sound like you, the Skilled Trades and this AYB Playbook are not for you.

## —————— CHAPTER 2 REPLAY ——————
### AYB Playbooks Are for You, If . . .

AYB Playbooks are for you if you are one of the following:

» The Newcomers—those entering the workforce for the first time

» The Veterans—those entering the civilian workforce after their military service

» The Restarters—those looking to change or reestablish their career path

» The Upgraders—those already working in or are entrepreneurs in a Skilled Trade, who want to "take it to the next level"

AYB Playbooks are for you, if . . .

» You just won't quit when things get tough
» You commit to completing projects with an eye for doing quality work

# CHAPTER 3

# The AYB Mental Framework

# YOU ARE AT YOUR BEST
## *when your head is firmly in the game.*

---

*The biggest mistake that you can make is to believe that you're working for somebody else. Job security is gone. The driving force of a career must come from the individual. Remember: Jobs are owned by the company, you own your career.*

—EARL NIGHTINGALE

---

## IT ALL BEGINS WITH "YOU, INC."

Wherever you are in your career, I would like to ask you to look at yourself as a business called "**You, Inc.**" This is the first element of the AYB mental framework and it applies whether you are someone looking to start a Skilled Trades career, or you are a long-time employee. You are "You, Inc." If your name is "Adam," then think in terms that this AYB Playbook is all about helping "Adam, Inc." be successful.

In Part 2 of this AYB Playbook, You, Inc. will represent you as an employee.

✓ You, Inc. has services to sell: Your skills, experience, professionalism and work product

✓ You, Inc.'s clients pay you for your services: Your employer and customers

✓ You, Inc.'s success is built on execution: Your reputation for high quality work

Here is a direct quote from James M., an excellent contractor and small business owner in Kansas, one of the AYB Subject Matter Experts that I believe hits the mark 100 percent.

---

*Everyone is replaceable. The only way to become less replaceable is to be better, to work harder and to always be improving your craft. Don't be afraid to outwork everyone around you every day, all day long without looking for recognition. It will come—do not worry.*

✓ *Commit yourself to outwork everyone around you*

✓ *Commit yourself to improve your Craftsmanship*

✓ *Commit yourself to always deliver quality and value to your crew, to your employer and to your client*

*Recognition and all that goes along with it will come. Why? Simple. It will come because you will have no competition and your reputation will pay you back many, many times over.*

---

This AYB Playbook is, in essence, You, Inc.'s business plan for success in the Skilled Trades. Developing a business plan before launching a new business is always an invaluable exercise. For our purposes, we will focus on the concept that you and your career represent a business called "You, Inc." and your plan for success is this AYB Playbook.

In Part 3 of this AYB Playbook, we will discuss how you can launch a small business as a self-employed Craftsman. At that point, I will ask you to broaden your definition of "You, Inc." to include you being self-employed and growing your new small business.

## You, Inc.

| Your Services | Your Clients | Your Success |
|---|---|---|
| Skills | Customers | Execution |
| Experience | Employer | Reputation |
| Professionalism | Co-Workers | Quality Work |
| Work Product | Vendors | |
| Time | | |

*Each of us need to live by our chosen core principles to be happy and successful in whatever we do. Pick the best ones for you and stick with them.*

—LARRY S., SMALL BUSINESS OWNER, SEATTLE

## 3P+A = PEOPLE, PERFORMANCE, PROFESSIONALISM & ATTITUDE

The next AYB Mental Framework concept that I want to ask you to internalize is: 3P+A, which stands for: **People, Performance, Professionalism & Attitude.**

The first "P" is always: **PEOPLE**

✓ You, Inc.'s success depends on how well you work with other people

✓ You must be able to communicate with and listen to other people

◊ *Commit to always give your best efforts toward building solid positive relationships with the people around you*

The next "P" is: **PERFORMANCE**

✓ You, Inc.'s success depends on the quality of You, Inc.'s work

✓ You must meet, and whenever possible, exceed expectations

◊ *Commit to always give your best efforts toward delivering the highest quality work product that you are able offer*

The final "P" is: **PROFESSIONALISM**

✓ You, Inc.'s success depends on your commitments made and met

✓ You must do what you commit to doing, by when you committed to having it completed, in the manner you committed to doing it, and done with the highest personal integrity

◊ *Commit to always give your best efforts toward being a professional in your behavior, performance and appearance always representing You, Inc.*

The Three Ps are all supported by "A" which stands for: **ATTITUDE**

- ✓ You, Inc.'s success depends on your best attitude—every day, all day long
- ✓ You must recognize that only you can control your attitude and how you react to everything you deal with on a daily basis

- ◊ *Commit to always try to keep a positive, proactive, "can-do" attitude toward whatever comes your way*
  - • I say, "try" because I know that it is a very hard thing to do all the time. Just know that the more you try the better you will become at having that positive, proactive, "can-do" attitude when it really counts.

## SUCCESS WITH 3P+A

Success in anything depends on many factors—some can be controlled, and some cannot. The factors that cannot be controlled are best left to luck, fate and solid planning to protect your downside. However, for those factors that you can control, you owe it to yourself to always keep the following top of mind:

### Only you can control your effort and your attitude— no matter what comes.

Remember, there are many things that can and will happen throughout your day that you cannot control. However, there are two things that you can control that will make all the difference in the success of You, Inc.

✓ *Only you can control the **effort** you put into your success*
- Are you putting in your best efforts toward your:
    ◊ People?
    ◊ Performance?
    ◊ Professionalism?

✓ *Only you can control your **attitude***
- Are you letting the "little stuff" of life get in the way of You, Inc.'s success?
- Remember: A moment of temper takes days to repair

Throughout your career, you need to recognize that the effort you put forth in every task and interaction builds and impacts your reputation as a Craftsman.

✓ You control how you choose to interact with people in the workplace. Differentiate yourself by how you treat and how well you work with:
- Your employer
- Your company's clients
- Your co-workers
- Your employees
- Your vendors

✓ You control the quality of each task and job you complete. Differentiate yourself with your consistently superior performance and "can-do" attitude

✓ You control the image you give of yourself and your company with each interaction you have when you are on and off the job. Differentiate yourself through your professionalism and your positive attitude

✓ You control how you react to what life throws your way. Everyone notices how you deal with the good, the bad and the ugly. Differentiate yourself with your positive attitude above all else

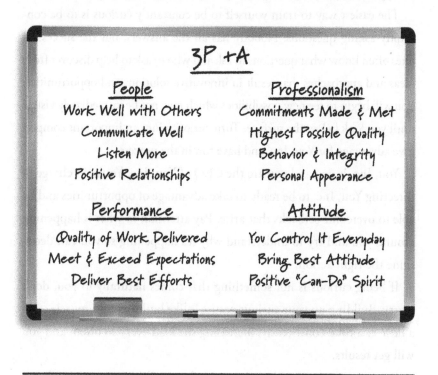

## 3P +A

### People
Work Well with Others
Communicate Well
Listen More
Positive Relationships

### Professionalism
Commitments Made & Met
Highest Possible Quality
Behavior & Integrity
Personal Appearance

### Performance
Quality of Work Delivered
Meet & Exceed Expectations
Deliver Best Efforts

### Attitude
You Control It Everyday
Bring Best Attitude
Positive "Can-Do" Spirit

*I have no special talents. I am only passionately curious.*

—ALBERT EINSTEIN

## CURIOSITY: AN IMPORTANT STATE OF MIND

There's one more letter to think about as you work on You, Inc., and that is "C" for curiosity. As kids we were always wondering and asking why, or what, or how things work or happen. Keeping that curiosity in what's going on around you will give you the opportunity to continue to learn and cultivate new ideas. Curiosity is the engine that drives innovation.

Curiosity keeps your mind active and allows you to turn ideas into action. There is something very satisfying that comes with identifying an opportunity and coming up with a solution.

The easiest way to train yourself to be constantly curious is to be constantly asking questions. Nobody has all the answers, but the successful ones often know what questions to ask and who to ask to help discover fresh ideas and approaches that result in innovative solutions and opportunities. You will begin to see new possibilities which may not be immediately visible until you look below the surface. Turn curiosity into an important competitive advantage for You, Inc. and have fun in the process.

You, Inc. is you and you are the CEO of You, Inc. You're in charge of directing You, Inc. to be ready to take advantage of opportunities and be able to overcome setbacks that arise. Pay attention to what is happening around you and try to understand why it's happening so you can determine the right action.

If being curious is not something that comes naturally to you, don't worry. Building up your curious nature is like building up a muscle—do a little at a time consistently, increasing the load every so often, and you will get results.

For instance, start with trying to understand the opportunity for an HVAC/R Technician in your local market. Here are a few examples of questions that you can ask yourself:

- ✓ Is economy in your town growing or shrinking? Is it likely to turn soon?
  - • The answer will help guide your decisions on whether to pursue you career as an HVAC/R Technician in your town or if you need to move somewhere else
- ✓ Are there a lot of new construction sites popping up as you drive around town?

- • If yes, that means that there will be a lot of job opportunities in your area
- ✓ Which contractors seem to have more signs up on job sites and have more trucks on the roads showing off their business logo on the doors?
  - • These are the contractors that you should contact first in your job search, as they're most likely to be in need of more HVAC/R Technicians sooner

Let your imagination guide your questions and answers to learn more about whatever you believe is important to You, Inc.'s future success. In the coming chapters in this AYB Playbook, there will many other questions that will prompt your curiosity. When you come up with questions you can't answer, ask someone, or take out your smartphone and do a quick Google search, or challenge yourself to figure it out.

Imagine all of the ways that You, Inc. will benefit by you actively directing your curiosity to your career. Think about how valuable it will be to your career to always be actively seeking out new things—new skills to do the job, new materials to use, or new approaches to old problems—to learn and master. Be curious, engage your mind, take action and enjoy the ride.

## FUTURE-PROOF YOUR LIFE WITH A SKILLED TRADE CAREER

The uncertainty of life is one of the only real constants that we all have to deal with no matter where we live. Our local, state and national economies will continue to go through their cycles of ups and downs. Businesses will thrive or fail as they always have and always will. Employees will continue to be laid off or outsourced or downsized depending on any number of factors.

There may be little you can do to stop life from presenting you and your family whatever economic difficulties may come due to the next down cycle. However, you do have it in your power to decide how you will meet and overcome the obstacles brought about by that next downturn.

The law of supply and demand has a lot to do with whether you can find the job you want and how much you will get paid in your local market. The growing Skills Gap across the country means that there is an ever-growing demand for people with the right skills and experience to filled needed, open jobs that pay rising middle-class salaries. Even in the depths of the most recent major recession, there were still millions of unfilled jobs across the US that were readily available to folks with the skills and experience to do them. When times are good, prepare yourself with skills, training and experience to ride out the next downturn.

Future-proof your career by acquiring the skills and experience—and adopting the mindset of a Craftsman in the Skilled Trades. Your skills and experience are portable and likely to be very much in demand somewhere else in the US. Your reputation and attitude as a Craftsman will serve to protect your downside when your economic picture unexpectedly changes. Your options are only limited by the requirements you place on where to look for your next opportunities.

---

*Being a Craftsman means you have valuable skills and experience. It means that "this" is more than a job. This is your profession— your calling—your mission.*

—GARTH B., CONTRACTOR, ATLANTA

---

## AT YOUR BEST AS A CRAFTSMAN*

In the Skilled Trades, you have a choice every day:

✓ Learn the skills and do the work to have **a job** to earn a paycheck

– or –

✓ Learn the skills and do the work to become **a Craftsman** to build a career on a foundation of delivering the highest quality work product, while raising your value with your employer/your customer

**At Your Best** is about choosing what is right for you at any given point in your life and career. Whether your choice is to ensure that you can always find a job that comes with a solid paycheck or it is to build a career that over time can potentially be turned into a small business, the Skilled Trades can be your path. This AYB Playbook is designed to help you make that happen no matter where you live in the US and no matter where you are in your work life. There are over **6 million unfilled jobs** out there right now and one of those can very well be yours!

Making the choice to become a **Craftsman**, however, goes hand-in-hand with being committed to be **At Your Best**. With the mindset of a Craftsman, your focus every day is on improving your skills so that your work product is always of the highest quality. That is a "win" for everyone—for you, for your employer and for your customers. Adopting the mindset of a Craftsman means:

✓ Greater satisfaction and pride from what you do
✓ A reputation built on delivering the highest quality work product
✓ The opportunity to maximize your earnings on any job
✓ Standing apart from your competition for any job at any level

✓ Becoming an employee that is sought after and who employers want to keep and help grow in skills and value to their company

## Mindset of a Craftsman

Reputation
Job Satisfaction and Pride
Highest Quality Work Product
Stand Above the Competition
Highly Valued Employee
Maximize Earnings
Integrity

*AYB Playbooks and www.AtYourBest.com use the term "Craftsman" instead of a generic or gender-neutral term because it is long-accepted and commonly understood to mean "a person who is highly skilled at a trade." Please accept this convention to be brief and to minimize confusion. Thank you.

## AT YOUR BEST AS A WOMAN IN THE SKILLED TRADES

The Skilled Trades afford women tremendous opportunities to build fruitful, long-lasting and well-paying careers. The reality of the "Skills Gap" and the resulting shortfall of more than six million unfilled jobs across the US, makes gender in hiring—in the workplace and in the question of which career path to pursue—as irrelevant as it should have always been.

Growing the ranks of women in the Skilled Trades needs to be an overriding priority for employers, educators and public officials if we ever hope to overcome The Skills Gap. The dual, societal stigmas of downplaying the value of a career in the Skilled Trades along with dismissing the notion of women in the Skilled Trades need to die quick and permanent deaths. As a country and as an economy, we cannot allow more than 50 percent of our population to be relegated to the sidelines when such opportunities exist to fundamentally change the lives of so many individuals and their families.

✓ Being **At Your Best** means focusing on what's truly important to creating the best You, Inc. in the Skilled Trade of your choice—for you, for your family and for your employer and/or your client
✓ Being **At Your Best** means working hard to put yourself in the best position to maximize your earning potential and to deliver the highest quality work product at each stage of your career
✓ Being **At Your Best** means knowing that a person's character and performance is all that matters

As a woman considering the Skilled Trades, know that you have the opportunity to be at the forefront of a much-needed paradigm shift. Skills and experience have no gender. It all comes down to being able to do the job well and being **At Your Best**.

## CHAPTER 3 REPLAY
### The AYB Mental Framework

» Begin by thinking of yourself as a business called You, Inc.
  • You, Inc. has services to sell—your time and work product
  • You, Inc. has clients who pay for your services—your employer and customers
  • You, Inc.'s success is built on execution and high-quality work
» The only way to become more highly valued and less replaceable is to be better, work harder and always be improving your craft
» 3P+A is a critical **At Your Best** mental framework concept
  • People—Your success depends on how well you communicate, listen and work with other people
  • Performance—Your success depends on the quality of your work and whenever possible on exceeding expectations
  • Professionalism—Your success depends on your doing what you commit to doing, when you committed to doing it, in the manner you promised, with the highest personal integrity
  • Attitude—Your success depends on you bringing your very best, positive, can-do attitude every day, all day
» Only you can control your effort and your attitude
» Become a Craftsman by building your career on solid reputation for always delivering the highest quality work product
  • Stand apart from the competition
  • Maximize your earning potential

# PART 2:

# AT YOUR BEST AS AN HVAC/R TECHNICIAN: BECOMING A WORLD-CLASS PLAYER

Now that we have laid the foundation for the balance of this AYB Playbook, let's move on to what it takes to become a successful HVAC/R Technician and build a great career. Part 2 is divided into three subparts, which correlate with the stages that a world-class athlete might go through to reach their highest potential. They first must choose the sport that is right for them and to which they fully commit to becoming the best that they can be. Then, they learn, practice and execute the skills and experience they need to compete and excel. Finally, they use that foundation of education, skills and experience along with the mental focus to become the best at their chosen sport that they can be to rise above their competition.

**Becoming a World-Class Player**

Skills & Experience + Mental Focus & Discipline

Learn    ->    Practice    ->    Execute

and Repeat . . . and Repeat . . . and Repeat

Now, consider that you and You, Inc. are that world-class athlete in the making. Part 2 of this AYB Playbook lays out the three stages of You, Inc. becoming a Craftsman HVAC/R Technician:

A) Becoming an HVAC/R Technician is "Right" for You, Inc.:
   Chapter 4 will provide you with:
   ✓ An overview of a career as an HVAC/R Tech
   ✓ A discussion of why and how to become an HVAC/R Tech
   ✓ A view of the career options that exist for HVAC/R Technicians
   ✓ A breakdown of the earning potential for HVAC/R Techs

B) Must-have education, skills, and experience for You, Inc. to excel as an HVAC/R Technician: Chapter 5 and Chapter 6 will present:
   ✓ A breakdown of the steps to becoming an HVAC/R Technician
   ✓ Local and online resources that you can use anywhere in the US to access the foundational education and training that you will need to succeed

✓ A roadmap to help you find work as an HVAC/R Tech so
you can practice and skills and build your career as an
HVAC/R Tech

C) Leveraging high-level execution and mental focus, You, Inc.'s
path to becoming a Craftsman: Chapter 7 and Chapter 8 will
lay out:
   ✓ A concrete set of actions to take and understandings to internalize to ensure You, Inc.'s success throughout your career
   ✓ Insights and advice from folks we all admire to help you keep
   or regain a positive mental focus and to be **At Your Best** no
   matter what may be going on

# CHAPTER 4

# Career Overview: HVAC/R Technician

## YOU ARE AT YOUR BEST
### *when you know why you want to set a specific goal for yourself and what reaching that goal will do for you.*

---

*There is always something more to learn in this field to make you better. They say, "information is power" but in HVAC, information is everything when combined with experience. Take every chance to learn about your craft.*

*—BRAD S., HVAC TECH, WASHINGTON STATE*

---

## CAREER OVERVIEW: HVAC/R TECHNICIAN

HVAC/R Technicians work on the heating, ventilation, air conditioning and refrigeration systems that control the temperature and airflow and quality in residential, commercial and public buildings. Specifically, the "R" in HVAC/R refers to Refrigeration Technicians that also work on commercial refrigeration systems that store and/or transport perishable foods, medicines, etcetera.

HVAC/R Technicians install, assemble or repair the furnaces, heat pumps, air conditioning units and cooling systems in buildings. HVAC/R

Technicians follow blueprints, technical drawings and specifications to install the required ductwork, vents, pumps, water and fuel supply lines as well as any other associated components. Given the critical importance and potential issues and costs of improperly completed work, HVAC/R Technicians must be highly trained and skilled.

## WHY BECOME AN HVAC/R TECHNICIAN?

The shortage of HVAC/R Technicians mirrors the growing shortfall across the US in all the Skilled Trades. It is real and significant at all job levels. The average age across the Skilled Trades in the US is fifty-five years old. Retirement is right around the corner and not enough young HVAC/R Technicians are coming up the ranks. Therefore, once you've acquired the skills, training and experience as an HVAC/R Tech, you will also have the flexibility to decide where you want to work and live. Your skills are portable, and they are always in demand.

As an HVAC/R Tech, you can choose to work as an employee for any number and types of employers, or you can choose to strike out on your own and be your own boss. You are only limited by your abilities, your ambition and your personal circumstances.

## HVAC/R TECHNICIAN: JOB RESPONSIBILITIES

HVAC/R Technicians have a wide variety of responsibilities depending on the specific role and job. At minimum, an HVAC/R Tech must be able to effectively:

✓ Install, assemble or repair furnaces, heat pumps, dehumidifiers and air conditioning units with associated wiring and controls
✓ Study and follow blueprints, drawings and building codes to ensure proper fabrication and placement of ductwork in building

✓ Maintain and adjust HVAC and refrigeration equipment and associated blowers, burners, thermostats, electrical circuits, controls and other components

✓ Testing performance on equipment to ensure each unit operates safely and at peak output and cost efficiency

✓ Rework, reroute and repurpose existing HVAC/R systems to properly address a new client need

✓ Direct other workers on proper layout, sheet metal cutting, preassembly and installation of ductwork

## HVAC/R TECHNICIAN: MINIMUM REQUIRED SKILLS & ABILITIES

Becoming a successful HVAC/R Technician first requires that you acquire the minimum set of skills and experience to even be allowed on a jobsite. We will discuss how you learn those skills and gain that experience a bit later. For now, consider the following list as a bare-bones checklist of what you will need to master:

✓ Solid comprehension of reading and math

✓ Be detail oriented and aware of work and surroundings

✓ Troubleshooting, problem solving and reasoning skills

✓ Knowledge of machines and tools, including their use and maintenance

✓ Knowledge of materials, methods and tools involved in construction

✓ Knowledge and use of principles in precision technical plans, blueprints, drawings and models

✓ Read and understand work-related manuals and documents

✓ Install equipment, wiring, etcetera, to meet technical specifications

✓ Effective workplace communication skills: both verbal and written
✓ Time management to complete tasks within expected period
✓ Work and interact well with others
✓ Concentrate on tasks without being distracted
✓ Consider the cost versus benefits of doing something before doing it
✓ Certified, comprehensive understanding of requirements set forth in EPA Section 608 of the Clean Air Act of 1990 as well as EPA R-410A for Refrigeration Technicians

## HVAC/R TECHNICIAN: WORK CONDITIONS

As you can imagine, the work conditions and jobsite requirements vary widely for every HVAC/R Technician, on every site, every day and throughout the workday. Still, you can expect some combination of the following:

**Work Site Conditions:**
✓ Work done outdoors with very high and low temperatures
✓ Work done indoors in cramped, close quarters regardless of conditions
✓ Hazardous equipment: hand and power tools and heavy equipment
✓ Hazardous materials: glues, solvents and fuels
✓ Hazardous heights: ladders, scaffolding and unstable, high places
✓ Required to wear protective clothing and accessories
✓ High and uncomfortable noise levels
✓ Early start times and often late finish times of a typical workday

**Physical Demands:**

- ✓ Lift, pull, push, carry and hold heavy items throughout the workday
- ✓ Use and maneuver hand and power tools in all angles
- ✓ Bend, stand and walk all day, often carrying heavy items
- ✓ Be physically active all day without limitation or getting tired
- ✓ Kneel, crawl, stoop and crouch in confined spaces
- ✓ Maintain balance while in unstable position for extended time
- ✓ Dexterity to accomplish difficult manual tasks in confined spaces

## HVAC/R TECHNICIAN: EARNING POTENTIAL

Your potential income as a skilled HVAC/R Technician will vary according to each local market and depending on your skill/experience level and specialization. **At Your Best** will continue to stress that by adopting and truly internalizing the mindset of a Craftsman, you will be able to maximize your income as an HVAC/R Technician.

Given the growing nationwide demand for HVAC/R Techs, you can look at the "national average income" levels a simply a reference point—a starting point. Averages are just that: the midpoint between the highs and the lows. Leave the "lows" and "medians" to someone else. Focus on the highs of being **At Your Best**. Be confident that your unfailing commitment to be **At Your Best**—to deliver the highest quality work product you can, always having a great attitude about your craft and job—will put you at the high end of the wage scale in quick order.

**2016 US National Average Income for an HVAC/R Technician:**

| | |
|---|---|
| High Income: | $73,350 |
| Median Income: | $45,910 |
| Low Income: | $28,440 |

Source: US Dept. of Labor–2016

However, rather than wasting your time discussing average national income levels that do not really apply to you, the following walks you through the easiest, fastest way I found to see what you can earn as an HVAC/R Technician, wherever you may live in the US using www .CareerOneStop.org

As of this writing, the CareerOneStop process for finding the income ranges for HVAC/R Tech-related careers near you is:

1. Go to www.CareerOneStop.org
2. Click on "Toolkit"
3. Under "Wages" click on "Salary Finder"
4. Enter "HVAC" or "Refrigeration" in "Search by Occupation"
5. Enter where you live or want to move in "Location"
6. Click on "Search"
7. If you only see the ranges for United States, just enter another, larger city close to the location you are considering

**AYB Quick Tool:** Go to www.AtYourBest.com and click on "**AYB Quick Tools**" where you will find a link **Salary Finder**. The instructions attached to this AYB Quick Tool link will always be up to date and ready to use.

## HVAC/R TECHNICIAN: YOUR CAREER OPTIONS

As a skilled HVAC/R Technician, you have a wide variety of industries and specializations you can pursue. You can work for someone else, choose to be a union member or independent, non-union HVAC/R Technician, or you can strike out on your own.

You also have several career paths available to you to follow, each of which are equally well-paying and very much in demand. Each is a specialization and Skilled Trade in and of itself, so you would have to expand your training and certifications accordingly. You can consider:

- ✓ Residential Air Conditioning and Heating
- ✓ Light Commercial Air Conditioning and Heating
- ✓ Commercial Refrigeration
- ✓ "Green" Heating Systems, including:
    - • Solar
    - • Geothermal
    - • Hydronics

## BECOMING AN HVAC/R TECHNICIAN: IS IT FOR YOU?

If you were wondering, this is one of the "Kitchen Table Moments" that will lead you to a very important decision. You need to do some self-reflection to decide whether becoming an HVAC/R Technician is right for you. There are no shortcuts.

You know at least the basics needed to become an HVAC/R Tech. Still, it would make a lot of sense for you to explore and understand more fully what it takes to be successful. Here are some avenues you might consider in deciding if a career as an HVAC/R Technician is for you:

**Friends & Family**    Ask around. Someone you know probably is or knows a successful HVAC/R Technician who would be happy to answer your questions about what it is like, what it takes and how to go about it.

**YouTube**    Sit back and watch some videos. There are countless videos available to you that can provide insights to any aspect of the HVAC/R profession. Take advantage of all that free advice! You can also check out additional valuable information on video and how-to sites like: Vimeo, WikiHow, eHow and Instructables.

**Local Union Office**    Visit the local union office. Given the shortage of skilled HVAC/R Technicians across the US, you will find the local union office is happy to help you learn more.

**Assessment Testing**    Take a skills and interest assessment test. There are many ways to undergo skills and interest assessment testing. Whether at school or online or at a local employment agency office or some other location, these assessment tests are easy and quick to take. There are no right or wrong answers. The results simply give you an insight to interests and careers you might consider pursuing further.

Here are a couple of assessment tests that you can take right now:

**O*NET Interest Profiler on My Next Move:**
✓ Go to www.MyNextMove.org
✓ Simply click on "Next" at the lower left and follow the directions
✓ By responding to a series of easy-to-answer questions, at the end you will be presented with a number of possible career options that fit your interests

**Interest Assessment and Skills Matcher on CareerOneStop:**

✓ Go to www.CareerOneStop.org
✓ Under "Explore Careers" click on "Self-Assessments"
✓ Now, follow the directions for the "Interest Assessment" and the "Skills Matcher"
✓ You get the results right after you answer the last question

## —————— CHAPTER 4 REPLAY ——————
## Career Overview: HVAC/R Technician

» HVAC/R Techs are critical contributors to the building trades and the quality of life of everyone in the US
» The skills and experience required to become a successful HVAC/R Technician are gained over time from working on many projects and jobsites. They are built on a foundation of basic knowledge and abilities that every HVAC/R Tech should have, including:
  • Solid understanding of basic math
  • Extensive training and understanding of the techniques, principles and requirements of the trade
  • Effective workplace communication skills, both verbal and written
  • Reasoning and problem-solving skills

» When deciding on whether becoming an HVAC/R Technician is for you, consider:

- Asking your friends and family, who may be HVAC/R Technicians themselves or be in the Skilled Trades or know someone who is

- Using YouTube and the Web to gain further insights on becoming an HVAC/R Tech

# CHAPTER 5

# Your Path to Becoming an HVAC/R Technician

# YOU ARE AT YOUR BEST
## *when you know the steps you need to take to accomplish a goal and why they are important to realizing your goal.*

---

## HOW TO BECOME AN HVAC/R TECHNICIAN

The process of becoming a successful HVAC/R Technician happens over a number of years as you learn the necessary skills and gain experience to set yourself apart as a true Craftsman. You acquire those skills and experiences as you move through the stages of building a successful HVAC/R Tech's career. With a game plan and much practice, you can progress from the minor leagues into the pros. However, if you plan to be **At Your Best** in your career as an HVAC/R Tech, you should first think about getting a solid education.

The next few pages lay out the stages that you can expect to traverse as well as the education that you will need to build your career as an HVAC/R Technician. You will also learn how to find the types of educational and apprenticeship programs that will help kick-start your career.

## THE CAREER STAGES OF A "MASTER HVAC/R TECHNICIAN"

There are always exceptions to every rule, but in order for you to set realistic expectations, the information below gives you an idea of what it will take to build a career as a skilled HVAC/R Technician. There is no set, legal, educational requirements to enter the HVAC/R profession. Therefore, in theory you could find an employer and start as, say, a helper and work your way up.

You can try to do it on your own:

✓ Find and hire on with a reputable HVAC or commercial refrigeration company
✓ Train as an Apprentice hopefully under a "Master HVAC/R Technician"—and hopefully on a one-on-one basis
  • In some states you need a trainee license, which requires no prior experience or training to obtain. It is typically valid for at least twenty-four months and requires at twenty-four hours of coursework per year
✓ After three years, take the first-level Journeyman license exam
  • Allows you to work alone in HVAC/R

However, this is not be the most reliable path to be **At Your Best** as an HVAC/R Technician. Invest in building a solid foundation for You, Inc. Get your education and training.

First, to even consider the possibility of moving forward, you have to recognize that you must:

✓ Have a high school diploma or equivalent
✓ Be at least eighteen years old
✓ Be in good physical condition

In broad terms the career of an HVAC/R Technician can be broken down into four stages:

**Stage One:**   HVAC/R Technician's Helper/Trainee/
Pre-Apprentice

**Stage Two:**   Vocational Education/HVAC/R Technician
Apprentice

**Stage Three:**  Journeyman

**Stage Four:**   "Master HVAC/R Technician"

Your Progression as an HVAC/R Technician

Stage Four
"Master HVAC/R Technician"
Accomplished!

Stage Three
Journeyman HVAC/R Tech
Four to five Years

Stage Two
Vocational Education
Community College Education
HVAC/R Apprentice
Three to four Years

Stage One
HVAC/R Helper
Trainee
Pre-Apprentice
As Long as it Takes

## *Stage One: HVAC/R Technician's Helper/Trainee/ Pre-Apprentice*

Explore the idea of becoming an HVAC/R Technician in every way available to you.

- ✓ Consider becoming an HVAC/R Technician's helper—get your hands dirty and see if being an HVAC/R Technician right for you:
    1. Identify the HVAC and/or commercial refrigeration businesses in your town or area that you plan to approach and learn everything you can about them, the type of work they do and their competitors on Google
    2. Put together a straightforward three-five minute conversational explanation and description as to why you want to be a helper/laborer on their work sites. Be clear that you are committed to working hard, showing up on time and doing whatever it takes to learn what it is to become a successful HVAC/R Tech
    3. Practice your "pitch" until you are comfortable with what you want to say. Do it in front of a mirror a few times. You'll be amazed at how much you will learn and improve
    4. Now, take action—go to your future employer's office and ask for the job—and keeping taking action until you succeed
    5. You are **At Your Best**. You have a plan. Now, work your plan
- ✓ Watch as many YouTube videos related to all things HVAC and commercial refrigeration, as well as topics like math for the trades
- ✓ Talk to current or retired tradespeople of all types. If they have been in construction on any level, they will have invaluable insights
- ✓ Let your imagination run wild but definitely give it some thought

## THE PACT CERTIFICATE

PACT stands for Pre-Apprenticeship Certificate Training. If you can't enter an apprenticeship program because of your lack of experience or some other reason, you might consider starting out as a helper on a construction crew to learn what it takes to be an HVAC/R Technician while you earn a PACT certificate. You can contact your local employment office or building trades union hall for more details. Also, do not forget to ask others on the construction crew. Chances are that they can point you in the right direction and fastest path to getting your certificate.

### Time needed to complete PACT certificate:

Approximately three to twelve months depending on many factors including your knowledge starting out and your ability and commitment to learn what you need to move on to the next stage. The amount of time required to secure your certificate can also depends on how the program sponsor balances more or less on-the-job training versus more or less classroom training, as well as whether they have a job slot ready to take you on upon completion.

Admission requirements to apprenticeship programs are competitive. On-the-job learning as an HVAC/R Technician's helper to get yourself ready to secure a slot with an apprenticeship program will take a long time and you still cannot be sure you have all your bases covered. Instead of learning on the job, you should seriously consider getting more formalized pre-apprenticeship training at a vocational, technical school or local community college.

### *Stage Two:  Vocational Education and/or Apprenticeship*

With a high school diploma or its equivalent like the GED, you can enroll in a vocational, technical school or community college, which may or may not be associated with an apprenticeship program.

A vocational school education will require one to two years to earn your certification of completion. A community college Associate Degree will take two years to complete. And, the typical apprenticeship program will require four years to complete. In some cases, the apprenticeship program may be associated with a local vocational school or a community college, where they combine the educational and apprentice programs into one, so you need to research your local market. Each local program will be different but in many, many cases the cost to you may turn out to be *zero*. We will discuss how to go about how to find programs in your local area shortly.

Again, securing a slot in an apprenticeship program is competitive. They usually consist of four years of on-the-job training. You are paid well for the time that you spend on the job. You also spend at least 144 hours per year in classroom training. Some programs also rely on online coursework and/or via correspondence.

As part of the application process, at minimum, you will have one or more interviews and must meet the by state/by program specific prerequisites, including:

✓ Reading comprehension in English
✓ Understanding of basic math
✓ An aptitude for heating and cooling systems and for how things work mechanically generally
✓ Pass a drug test
✓ Must have a clean criminal record (to be licensed as an Apprentice)

Your apprenticeship will combine on-the-job training with classroom and/or online coursework. You'll be mentored and supervised by seasoned HVAC/R Techs and you will earn an hourly wage for your work.

By the end of your apprenticeship, you will be trained and qualified to perform a wide range of HVAC and refrigeration related tasks as a "Journeyman."

**Time needed to complete vocational or community college education:**
Up to two years.

**Time needed to complete HVAC/R apprenticeship:**
Four to five years, which may include the time spent earning the vocational school/community college degree.

## Stage Three: Journeyman

Having completed your apprenticeship, you will want to get licensed, which will be covered during your program. Licensing requirements differ from state to state and even by municipality so be sure to check the local licensing requirements as you move across the US. Some licensing prerequisites are:

- ✓ Proof that you have completed the minimum number of required years working in the industry as an Apprentice in good standing
- ✓ Passing the two primary Journeyman-level exams
- ✓ Local laws and building codes, which obviously differ accordingly

**Time needed as a Journeyman:**
Your choice based on your career goals as a Journeyman HVAC/R Tech. In other words, you can choose to remain a Journeyman for the rest of your career and do exceptionally well. Or, you can choose to continue gaining the skills and certification to become a "Master HVAC/R Technician."

## Stage Four: "Master HVAC/R Technician"

As a "Master HVAC/R Technician," you can work for another company or work for yourself as a contractor. Licensing requirements for additional education and experience beyond that of a Journeyman differ significantly from state to state.

### Time needed for a Master HVAC/R Specialist license:

Two to five years as a Journeyman, depending on the individual state and Master certification program(s).

---

*You just don't want to be that guy driving around with a hammer and saw looking to hopefully luck into a slot on a jobsite.*

—JAMES M., CONTRACTOR, KANSAS

---

## YOUR EDUCATION IS YOUR FOUNDATION

There are no substitutes for an education. True success in the Skilled Trades demands that you build a strong foundation with a solid education.

This does not mean that if you did not complete a formal, classroom education, you cannot consider a career in the Skilled Trades. It does, however, mean that you cannot hope to be successful in the Skilled Trades, unless—*at minimum*—you learn and are able to build on the basic education that is typically taught in high school.

It is never too late to learn what you need. Whether or not you have your high school diploma, or its equivalent, will be important to checking off that typical requirement for moving to the next step. However, even more important is that you actually learned the basics in math, reading and writing. So, even if you do not have a high school diploma, it is never too late. Get a high school equivalency certification. If you do not have a good understanding of basic math, reading and writing, it is never too late. Get a friend to help you; go on YouTube and watch tutoring videos; take a class; and/or go to a local school and ask for some guidance.

**The Hard Truth:** It is never too late but also remember, there are no shortcuts. You need to learn the basics in math, reading and writing or you will not succeed.

---

*The capacity to learn is a gift, the ability to learn is a skill, but the willingness to learn is a choice.*

—BRIAN HERBERT

---

## HIGH SCHOOL OR ITS EQUIVALENT

Entering any of the Skilled Trades requires you to learn and master a great many skills. Your ability to improve your standing amongst your competition in the job market depends on your ability to continue improving your skills and experience. It all starts with mastering certain basic skills that earn you a high school diploma; or, if you did not receive your diploma, by passing a high school equivalency (HSE) exam like the GED.

Simply earning a high school diploma or passing an HSE exam is only one step. While in high school, if Skilled Trade courses (noted below) are offered, you should take advantage of any opportunity to gain an understanding of the basics that you will need in the future. By way of a reminder, to really be in the best position to proceed to the next step of entering a vocational, technical school, community college and/or an apprenticeship program, you should have a solid understanding of:

- ✓ Math, including algebra
- ✓ English comprehension to be able to read technical documents
- ✓ Basic reading of blueprints and mechanical drawings
- ✓ Basic knowledge of use and maintenance of tools and machines
- ✓ Problem solving and reasoning skills

It is likely that given how things are evolving in our school systems around the US, some of these subjects will not be readily available to you. If these courses are not offered in your high school, or if you are getting your GED or if you are changing careers and learning a completely new trade, there is a GREAT resource at your fingertips: **the Khan Academy.**

## KHAN ACADEMY

The Web gives you access to a wide variety of free, instructional courses on almost any topic. When it comes to basic academic subjects like arithmetic, algebra and grammar, along with subjects like physics and chemistry, the Khan Academy is by far one of the best free resources on the Web. Do yourself a favor. If you feel that you need a bit of extra help with your core math skills or some other subject, visit the Khan Academy, sign up and take some refresher sessions at your own pace, in your own time—at no cost to you.

- ✓ Go to www.KhanAcademy.org
- ✓ Scroll down to see the subjects available at Khan Academy
- ✓ Each subject is broken down into short sessions and videos to build your understanding

## CAREERONESTOP: YOUR FIRST STOP FOR FINDING LOCAL RESOURCES

The CareerOneStop website is sponsored by the US Department of Labor. It offers the most comprehensive and updated information you will need to make your search for answers local and immediately actionable. In this AYB Playbook, you will be directed many times to go to CareerOneStop to access many valuable resources. You should seriously consider making www.CareerOneStop.org your "Go-To" resource and jumping-off point for the vast majority of questions that might come up as you build your career as an HVAC/R Technician.

"Local and actionable"—this is obviously important. You need to be able to find the answers, programs and assistance when you need them, but they need to be located as close to where you live. CareerOneStop lets you find them with the most up to date information. Here are just some of the topics that are covered:

- ✓ Interest and skills assessment
- ✓ Researching and comparing occupations
- ✓ Finding a local education, apprenticeship and training program
- ✓ Financial aid for your education and training
- ✓ Starting point for your local, state, regional or national job search
- ✓ Tools and guidance to improve your job-hunting skills
- ✓ Finding the right local, city or state agencies where you live or where you want to move

## VOCATIONAL, TECHNICAL SCHOOL VERSUS COMMUNITY COLLEGE

We have established the importance of you getting the education and skills needed to become a successful HVAC/R Technician. Once you have your high school diploma or its equivalent, you now have a choice.

Either you can be the person who starts from the ground up as a general laborer on work sites and taking your chances that you will learn what you need to progress, OR you can enroll in classes that will teach what you need to know to leapfrog that "ground-up" guy.

To be **At Your Best**, I would suggest that you really want to be the person doing the leapfrogging. Still, you have a choice to make. Which type of education is right for you: a vocational, technical school or a community college? Money and time are too precious to waste by not thinking through your objectives and then committing to the course of action that is right for you. You need to answer the following question: **What do I want to do with my degree?**

| VOCATIONAL, TECHNICAL SCHOOL | | COMMUNITY COLLEGE | |
|---|---|---|---|
| Pro | One- to two-year education programs leading to certification of completion | Pro | Two-year program to earn an Associate Degree with more local campuses |
| Pro | Coursework limited and designed for quicker access to specific local jobs | Pro | Coursework more flexible allowing more electives to explore more options |
| Pro | School ties to local businesses and unions with links to apprenticeships | Pro | School ties to broader array of local businesses due to wider offerings |
| Pro | Costs less than community college | Pro | Costs much less than four-year schools |
| Con | More trades-focused courses with few electives | Con | Fewer fast-to-work trades-focused coursework |
| Con | May not have local campus locations | Con | Some required courses less desirable |

Whether you choose a vocational, technical school or a community college, keep in mind that there are many financial assistance programs available and ready to help you. Whatever your financial situation, it should not be the reason for you to miss out on your education.

**AYB Quick Tool:** Go to www.AtYourBest.com and click on "**AYB Quick Tools**" where you will find a link to **Find Local Financial Aid.**

## FINDING THE RIGHT TYPE OF SCHOOL OR PROGRAM FOR YOU

As with everything nowadays, there are various ways to search for the right vocational, technical school for you. The following walks you through the easiest, fastest way I found to find a program near you, wherever you may live in the US, using www.CareerOneStop.org.

As of this writing, the CareerOneStop process for finding a vocational, technical school offering HVAC/R-related courses near you is:

1. Go to www.CareerOneStop.org
2. Click on "Find Training"
3. Enter "HVAC" or "Refrigeration" in "Occupation, school or program"
4. Enter where you live or want to move in "Location"
5. Click on "Search"

A second approach that you might consider in finding a local trade school offering "HVAC" or "Refrigeration" related courses near you is:

1. Go to www.Trade-Schools.net
2. Enter your zip code
3. In "Optional: Area of Study" scroll and click on "Skilled Trade"

4. In "Optional: Program" scroll and on the Skilled Trade of your choice

5. You can choose the venue for your studies either "Campus" or "Online" or "Both" or you can just click on "Search Now"

**AYB Quick Tool:** Go to www.AtYourBest.com and click on "**AYB Quick Tools**" where you will find the link **Find Local Training**. The instructions attached to this AYB Quick Tool link will always be up to date and ready to use.

## POST–9/11 GI BILL & VOCATIONAL EDUCATION

If you are a Veteran and you are considering entering the Skilled Trades, you—and qualified dependents, as well as the children and surviving spouse of a service member who died in the line of duty after September 10, 2001—are entitled to education benefits if:

✓ You qualify for any GI Bill **and**

✓ You have served on active duty for at least ninety days—with or without a break in service—after September 10, 2001
   • The percentage amount of the maximum available benefit that you qualify for depends on your length of time in active duty. For instance:
   • Ninety days = 40 percent of maximum amount
   • Three years+ = 100 percent of maximum amount

The benefits available to you include:

✓ Tuition in-state schools up to $22,805.34

✓ Money for housing (if you are in school more than half time)

✓ Money for books and supplies (up to $1,000 per school year)

To learn more about and apply for Post–9/11 GI Bill benefits to help you with your education:

1. Go to www.Vets.gov
2. Click on "Explore Benefits" and then click on "Education & Training"
3. Click on "GI Bill programs" and then click on "Post–9/11 GI Bill"

## APPRENTICESHIP: THE DEGREE THAT PAYS YOU

Apprenticeships combine on-the-job-training with specialized classes to give you the skills you need to begin your career as an HVAC/R Technician. An apprenticeship program will pay you for the work you actually perform on the jobsites, while being supervised by seasoned Journeymen and Craftsmen to help jump-start your career. Rather than paying for a four-year degree at a college or university and building up all that student debt, you are the one getting paid to learn.

The availability and types of apprenticeship programs and the organizations that offer them vary widely depending on where you live in the US. Programs are offered by a local or regional union office, or in conjunction with a vocational school or community college, or by a one or more local employer or trade association or by some other private or publicly funded group.

### Minimum Requirements to Apply for Apprenticeship:

Each apprenticeship program and every state may have slightly different set of minimum requirements; however, you should expect the following as the general minimum:

✓ Must be eighteen years of age
✓ High school graduate or GED equivalent
✓ Physically able to do the work required

✓ Applicants must provide copies of:
  • Current driver's license
  • Social Security card or other I-9 documentation
  • High school diploma, official transcript or GED
✓ Applicants will typically need to pass a drug test

## Length of an Apprenticeship Program:

✓ Sixty months depending on requirements set by each state and/or program sponsor

## Topic Areas Covered during Apprenticeship Program Include:

✓ Basic principles and concepts of electricity
✓ Basic principles of heating systems: oil, gas and electric
✓ Basic refrigeration and charging procedures
✓ Components of HVAC systems
✓ General HVAC theory
✓ Fundamentals of electricity
✓ Electric, gas and oil heat
✓ Basic electronics
✓ Refrigerant types and refrigerant oils
✓ Carbon monoxide and combustion analysis
✓ Building codes and safety practices
✓ Reading and interpreting blueprints and mechanical drawings
✓ Airflow and indoor air quality
✓ Installation, servicing and troubleshooting
✓ Venting and duct systems including soldering and brazing
✓ Installing, troubleshooting, repairing and maintaining existing HVAC/R systems

## *Your Wage Scale during Apprenticeship:*

As an Apprentice, you will be paid a percentage of the market rate being paid to a Journey-level HVAC/R Technician. The following provides you an example of how you would be paid as an Aapprentice. Your actual pay as an Apprentice will be determined by two factors in your specific local market: the market wages earned by Journeymen in your state, regional and/or local area and the wage scale percentages defined by the state or apprenticeship program sponsor.

To figure out how much you would be paid at each level as an Apprentice consider the following:

1.  As an example, assume a local market hourly wage for a Journeyman HVAC/R Tech is $38.00
2.  As you progress and are certified through each competency stage of your apprenticeship, your pay increases accordingly

| COMPETENCY STAGE IN APPRENTICESHIP | LENGTH OF TIME | PERCENTAGE OF JOURNEYMAN WAGE | YOUR HOURLY WAGE |
|---|---|---|---|
| 1 | 0–2,000 hours | 50 | $19.00 |
| 2 | 2,001–4,000 hours | 62.5 | $23.75 |
| 3 | 4,001–6,000 hours | 70 | $26.60 |
| 4 | 6,001–8,000 hours | 75 | $28.50 |
| 5 | 8,001–10,000 hours | 85 | $32.30 |

Along with earning an hourly wage, most apprenticeships will also provide health insurance and other benefits.

## FINDING THE APPRENTICESHIP PROGRAM FOR YOU

Again, using CareerOneStop, you can find the apprenticeship program closest to where you live or where you would like to live. As of this writing, the CareerOneStopg process for finding an apprenticeship program in HVAC/R near you is:

1. Go to www.CareerOneStop.org
2. Click on "Toolkit"
3. Under "Training" click on "Apprenticeship Finder"
4. Enter "HVAC" or "Refrigeration" in "Search by Occupation or Apprenticeship"
5. Enter where you live or want to move in "Location"
6. Click on "Search"

You can also find additional information on securing a local apprenticeship slot by going directly to some of the organizations that regularly offer classes. Go to the websites below or visit a local office to find out more about their apprenticeship programs.

✓ United Association of Plumbers, Fitters, Welders and HVAC Service Techs (www.UA.org)
✓ Plumbing-Heating-Cooling Contractors Association (www.PHCCWeb.org)
✓ International Training Institute (www.SheetMetal-ITI.org)

**AYB Quick Tool:** Go to www.AtYourBest.com and click on "**AYB Quick Tools**" where you will find a link to **Find an Apprenticeship**. The instructions attached to this AYB Quick Tool link will always be up to date and ready to use.

## CERTIFICATIONS FOR YOU AS A CRAFTSMAN

As you build your career as a Craftsman HVAC/R Technician, you may choose to get outside validation for your skills and experience that you have acquired. Not only will doing so set you apart from your competition, it will allow you to maximize your earning potential.

Use CareerOneStop to find the certifications that can help you advance in your craft as an HVAC/R Technician:

1. Go to www.CareerOneStop.org
2. Click on "Toolkit"
3. Under "Training" click on "Certification Finder"
4. Enter "HVAC" or "Refrigeration" in "Search by Certification Name, Organization, Industry or Occupation"
5. Click on "Search"

A second approach to finding certification programs that can help you validate your enhanced skills and experience as a Craftsman:

1. Go to www.NCCER.org (National Center for Construction Education & Research)
2. Scroll over "Program Resources" and then "Crafts/Titles" and then click on "Construction & Maintenance"
3. Scroll through the "Search Titles and Disciplines" until you find "HVAC" or "Refrigeration" and click
4. Read through the section to identify the available assessments and certifications as well as local facilities and online resources

Finally, you will also want to determine whether your state requires any specific licenses in order to find work. If you have any questions whether you need a state license, the most comprehensive website and quickest, easiest way to find answer is:

1. Go to: www.ContractorQuotes.us/get-contractors-license
2. On the left, select the State that interests you and click on it
3. Scroll through the resulting web page and do your research on your State's licensing requirements

**AYB Quick Tool:** Go to www.AtYourBest.com and click on "**AYB Quick Tools**" where you will find a link to **Find Certifications**. The instructions attached to this AYB Quick Tool link will always be up to date and ready to use.

## AT YOUR BEST AS A UNION MEMBER

Becoming a member of a trade union is an important personal decision as well as an economic one that you should consider. Many local job opportunities are only available to you if you are a union member in good standing. As a union member, you have the opportunity for:

✓ Higher negotiated, standard pay and wages
✓ Defined work hours
✓ Reliable set of benefits including retirement plans, health insurance, vacation and sick leave and tuition reimbursement
✓ Specified, controlled working conditions
✓ Wide variety of sponsored education, training and certifications

Visit your local union or trade association office and learn more. There should be no question in your mind that becoming a union HVAC/R Technician offers you world-class training, long-term income potential and job security that will not be immediately available to you as an independent, non-union HVAC/R Technician. You might find that for you and your personal situation, the benefits of being a union member outweigh the member dues and the benefits of remaining independent.

You can also find a great deal of value in joining a related trade union or association. For more information, contact them directly at their closest local office or visit and study their website:

- ✓ United Association of Plumbers, Fitters, Welders and HVAC Service Techs (www.UA.org)
- ✓ Associated Builders & Contractors (www.ABC.org)
- ✓ Associated General Contractors of America (www.AGC.org)
- ✓ National Association of Building Trades Unions (www.NABTU.org)
- ✓ National Association of Women in Construction (www.NAWIC.org)
- ✓ Helmets to Hardhats (www.HelmetsToHardhats.org)

## AT YOUR BEST AS A MILITARY VETERAN

The Skilled Trades offer military Veterans a wide range of occupations to choose from when transitioning back into civilian life. The process of knowing how and where to start the process of moving into a Skilled Trades career after serving in the military is no doubt a challenge.

As a starting point, Veterans should visit www.CareerOneStop.org/ Veterans—the Veteran and Military Transition Center on the US Department of Labor's website. The Veteran and Military Transition Center is "a one-stop website for employment, training and financial help after military service."

The Veteran and Military Transition Center offers Veterans a go-to location on the Web from which they can find local programs and resources for:

- ✓ Earning educational and professional certifications and licensing
- ✓ Financial aid for securing degrees, certifications and licensing

✓ Job search resources and skills training
  • Determining how your military work experience translates to the civilian workforce
✓ Access to Veterans' and family benefits and assistance
  • Unemployment benefits
  • Health care
  • Housing and energy
  • Food and family support
  • Financial and tax counseling
  • Stress related counseling and support
  • Dedicated resources and programs for:
    ◊ Disabled Veterans
    ◊ Women Veterans
  • Finding military and other records

To learn more about the Veteran and Military Transition Center, do the following:

1. Go to www.CareerOneStop.org/Veterans
2. Depending on your interest or need, click on the appropriate link
   • Back to School
   • Job Search
   • Benefits and Assistance
   • Toolkit

**AYB Quick Tool:** Go to www.AtYourBest.com and click on "**AYB Quick Tools**" where you will find a link to **Resources for Veterans**. Websites are updated all the time. The instructions attached to this AYB Quick Tool link will always be up to date and ready to use.

## YOUTUBE IS YOUR FRIEND

YouTube is also a tremendous, free resource that you can turn to for instructional videos on all sorts of topics. Chances are that if you are interested in learning about something, someone has already made and posted a video detailing the specifics of that something.

### Make YouTube your best friend!

Whenever you have free time, go to www.YouTube.com and search for videos that give a better understanding of whatever topic interests you. For example, at the search field on the YouTube site type in:

- ✓ Repair HVAC or heating, ventilation, air conditioning, refrigeration
- ✓ Components of HVAC systems
- ✓ General HVAC theory
- ✓ Fundamentals of Electricity
- ✓ Essential tools and equipment used in HVAC
- ✓ Sheet metal basics
- ✓ Day in the life of an HVAC or refrigeration Apprentice

Each of these searches will result in several videos on the specific topic and several more on related topics that you can watch and expand your knowledge of HVAC/R.

There are also countless YouTube channels that you can subscribe to that go into further detail about any topic under the sun. Take advantage of the expert advice that is just waiting for you. Let your imagination run wild.

You can also check out additional valuable information on other online video and how-to sites like: Vimeo, WikiHow, eHow and Instructables.

## ───────── CHAPTER 5 REPLAY ─────────
## Your Path to Becoming an HVAC/R Technician

» The stages of a career as an HVAC/R Technician are:

  • Stage One—HVAC/R Tech's Helper/Trainee/Pre-Apprentice

  • Stage Two—Apprentice and/or Vocational Education

  • Stage Three—Journeyman

  • Stage Four—"Master HVAC/R Technician"

» Education is the foundation to your success

  • You must have a solid understanding of the basic subjects learned in high school or an equivalent program in math, reading comprehension and writing in English

  • Vocational, technical schools and community colleges can provide you cost-effective ways to further your education in topic areas that will serve you in finding your first job as an HVAC/R Technician and for the rest of your career

» Apprenticeship: the four-year education that pays you. Work while you learn to do things the right way from Journeymen and "Master HVAC/R Techs"

» The opportunities and benefits of joining a local trade union are significant and real. As you pursue your career as an HVAC/R Technician, you should consider whether joining a union is for you

» Use www.CareerOneStop.org to find information concerning a career as an HVAC/R Technician in your local and regional market anywhere in the US, such as:

  • Salary information

  • Educational programs and financial aid resources

  • Apprenticeships and other training programs

  • Veterans assistance programs

  • Certification programs

# CHAPTER 6

# Finding Work as an HVAC/R Technician

# YOU ARE AT YOUR BEST
*when you take control of finding your own path to your future, instead of just letting the future happen to you.*

---

*Happiness does not come from a job. It comes from knowing what you truly value, and behaving in a way that's consistent with those beliefs.*

—MIKE ROWE, TV PERSONALITY AND
SKILLED TRADES ADVOCATE

---

## FINDING WORK AS AN HVAC/R TECHNICIAN

You have laid the foundation. You have learned the skills. You have gotten the experience. Now, you want to get to work. Where do you turn to and what is your next step?

Every job search is difficult for the person searching for a job. And, every job search is different for every person depending on their abilities and local market conditions as well so many other factors too numerous to list here. Even so, you need to have a starting point. **Remember:** There are over 6 million unfilled jobs out there! Employers are looking for you!

## YOUR JOB SEARCH STARTING POINTS

Whether you are looking for work in your home town or some other place in the US, a good first step to get an idea of what is going on the local market you are interested in, is to do a quick online search.

- ✓ Go to www.CareerOneStop.org
- ✓ Under "Job Search" go to "Find a Job"
- ✓ Under "Job" enter "HVAC" or "Refrigeration" and the location under "Location"
- ✓ Scroll through the job opportunities

A second starting point that you should use along with your online search is to visit a local American Job Center (AJC) or affiliate. These are local workforce resource offices that can help you find out what jobs are out there right now. To find the closest AJC office:

- ✓ Go to www.CareerOneStop.org
- ✓ Under "Find Local Help" go to "Find an American Job Center"
- ✓ Enter the "Location" you desire and click "Search"
- ✓ Visit the local AJC office to learn about current job openings, as well as all the local job search resources available to you

## YOUR FULL-TIME JOB IS TO FIND A FULL-TIME JOB

The idea that to be **At Your Best** is about having a plan, falls apart if you do not also—**Work Your Plan.** No one can or will do it for you. It is up to you. Day in and day out, all day long, it is up to you. Your full-time job, until you find a full-time job, is to put in the time and do the work to find that job.

Take a look around your local area or where you plan to move. Learn the "lay of the land," learn who the players are and learn what kind of businesses they are. Make a plan of who you want to approach. Do your homework on each company that interests you:

- ✓ Who are the dominant players?
- ✓ Do they have a website?
- ✓ If they do, study up on them to see if you want to work there
- ✓ If they don't, is that a competitive disadvantage?
- ✓ What is their Better Business rating? Go to www.BBB.org and look them up
- ✓ Do they have reviews on Angie's List or Home Advisor? Go to www.AngiesList.com and www.HomeAdvisor.com to look up their ratings and read their customers' comments
  - How do they compare? What are their strengths and weaknesses?

## YOUR SKILLS ARE PORTABLE

**Remember, your skills as a skilled HVAC/R Technician are "portable."** That means that you are not limited by location. You have skills that are very much in demand in a lot of "somewhere elses" around the country. If your circumstances allow, use that to your advantage. Widen your search. Explore your options. Take your American Dream on the road.

## AYB STEPS & TOOLS TO FIND A GREAT JOB

Looking for a job can be difficult. It can be hard on the ego. It requires a thick skin to deal with the potential rejection. It is all those things, but it is also what you need to do to be **At Your Best**. Below describes a straightforward process that you can follow to get out there and put your best foot forward in looking for a job. At each step, you will find that there are tools, such as worksheets and templates on the www.AtYourBest .com site that can help you be better prepared.

✓ Put together a well-written **resume** that lays out your experience and technical skills

**AYB Quick Tool:** Go to www.AtYourBest.com and click on "**AYB Quick Tools**" where you will find a link to download a Microsoft Word file of **Resumes for the Skilled Trades**. The worksheet and examples are easy to modify and make your own.

✓ Put together a straightforward three to five minute **"elevator pitch"\*\*** or a conversational explanation/description of:
✓ the type of work and position that you are looking for
✓ why you have the skills and experience needed, coupled with
✓ the desire and commitment to work hard to deliver a quality work product on-time and on-budget and
✓ why you want to work for their company

\*\*Definition of "elevator pitch": Imagine that you get on an elevator with a potential boss and you have the thirty seconds to tell them about yourself and impress him or her on why you would be a great hire before one of you reaches your floor. In a sentence or two, why are you the best person for the job?

**Important note:** Be sure to practice your elevator pitch until you feel as comfortable and natural saying it as when you are having a simple conversation with a friend. If nothing else, do it in front of a mirror. I'm not kidding. You will learn a lot and it will all be useful in making you better at telling the You, Inc. story and impressing the listener.

**AYB Quick Tool:** Go to www.AtYourBest.com and click on "**AYB Quick Tools**" where you will find a link to a Microsoft Word file for **Elevator Pitch Worksheet**. The worksheet and instructions walk you through the process of creating your own elevator pitch.

✓ Put together a **plan of action** to contact your future employer

✓ Then, take action and keep taking action until you succeed

✓ You are **At Your Best**. You have a plan. Now, work your plan

**AYB Quick Tool:** Go to www.AtYourBest.com and click on "**AYB Quick Tools**" where you will find a link to a Microsoft Word file for **Job Search Action Plan**. The worksheet and instructions will help you quickly put together your plan for your job search with steps and timing.

## "FORCE MULTIPLIERS" & NETWORKING TO FIND A JOB

Networking is one of the most effective ways of finding a job. My belief is that to network effectively you need to focus on identifying and assembling a group of **force multipliers**. Force multipliers are those people that magnify or leverage your presence and impact far beyond what you might be able to do on your own. Examples of a force multiplier are:

✓ Friends or family who know or work for a local contractor in the construction in any of the Skilled Trades. Each contractor knows several more contractors and they are looking for great people

✓ Someone from your church or in your parents' group or on your softball team that is in a local builders' association or chamber of commerce. If not, go to the association's or chamber's offices, they will probably know of more than a few contractors looking for someone like you

✓ Hardware or building supplies and equipment vendors who serve local contractors in your community. Since successful contractors are always looking for their next great hire, they are always telling their vendors to "keep their eyes open for the right person"

Building your network of force multipliers, like everything else of value, takes time and effort. There are many books and articles on how to network your way to a new job. However, they all come back to a basic strategy that can be presented in four steps—with some **At Your Best** fine tuning. Consider the following:

### Step 1: Getting a Lay of the Land

**Objective of Step 1:** To create a comprehensive "lay of the land" in your local market of possible employers.

Start by asking yourself: Who are contractors or firms in the local market that have hired someone with your skills and positive attitude that you might want to work for? Your objective is to get a complete "lay of the land" of possible employers.

- ✓ Put together a complete list of the potential employers that you identify, along with as much contact information you find
- ✓ Spend some quality time on www.CareerOneStop.org to identify potential employers and then see if they have a website that you can review
- ✓ Do your research on the Web, or in the library, and by asking anyone you believe might know someone

### Step 2: Identify Possible Leverage Contacts

**Objective of Step 2:** To identify leverage points or contacts that might provide access to the possible employers on your Step 1 list.

Next, ask yourself: Who are all the other contractors and businesses that work with those prospective employers that you might want to work for?

✓ Put together another, separate list of each one you identify along with as much contact information you find

✓ Do your research on the Web, or in the library, and by asking anyone you believe might know someone

### Step 3: Identify Path to a Warm Lead-In

**Objective of Step 3:** To identify "warm" access point contacts for you to start your networking into the businesses you have identified in Steps 1 and 2. "Warm" contacts are those people who can give you access to the person you really want to meet with and possibly allow you to use their name or reference to facilitate your call or visit. A warm contact helps you avoid having to call or contact a person completely out of the blue with no introduction or prior context—typically referred to as a "cold call."

Now, ask yourself: Who are the people in your circle of acquaintances (your family, friends, friends-of-friends or simply possible, arms-length people connections) that might know a possible decision-maker or just a foot-in-the-door contact at those prospective employers OR at those leverage point businesses that you came up with on your Step 2 list?

✓ Put together one last list. This list will have the individual acquaintance along with who they might know—directly or indirectly—at the businesses you have identified in Steps 1 and 2

✓ If, after careful consideration, you do not have any acquaintances that might point you in the right direction, there is something you can do

✓ Ask yourself: Who do I need to meet that might know someone at either a Step 1 or Step 2 business? Then, set about meeting them

✓ Go to jobsites around your local area during lunchtime, be respectful of the work environment and try to strike up conversations with workers or the foreman on the job to ask for the assistance in identifying the correct person that you should contact

## Step 4: Be Your Own Full-Time Evangelist

**Objective of Step 4:** To actively and systematically communicate You, Inc.'s value proposition—*Why you are the best possible new employee for your chosen, target prospective employers*—as presented via your elevator pitch to as many people as you come in contact with in order to reach the decision-makers at your prospective, target employers.

Finally, put it all together by working backward from your lists:

✓ Give your elevator pitch to every person that you came up with in **Step 3** and ask them who they might know at the businesses on your Step 2 and Step 1 lists

✓ Then, give your elevator pitch to every person you can identify or meet from the businesses on your **Step 2** list to see if they can gain you access to those on your Step 1 list

✓ Finally, give your elevator pitch to every person you can identify or meet from the businesses on your **Step 1** list to see if they can gain you access to the hiring decision-maker(s)

Every time you give your elevator pitch, remember: If that person can't help you right then, ask them to keep their ears and minds open to anyone looking for someone fitting who you described in your elevator pitch. Also, if the opportunity presents itself, you REALLY want to also ask them for feedback on your elevator pitch to see if you might want to fine tune it in some way. Then, as they say, "if at first you don't succeed, try, try again" . . . then again . . . and again.

There is no doubt that there are millions of unfilled jobs throughout the US and, for sure, one of those jobs can be yours. The thing is that each job opportunity exists and is available in a specific local market. If that is your local market, it is up to you to put yourself in the best position for that employer to know that you could be the ideal employee for the job. You need to get the word out that you are that ideal employee. You need to be your own evangelist.

The ideal job that you have been looking for may be right around the corner but to get it, you have to beat out your competition. Your reputation, professionalism and your positive attitude will make the difference every time.

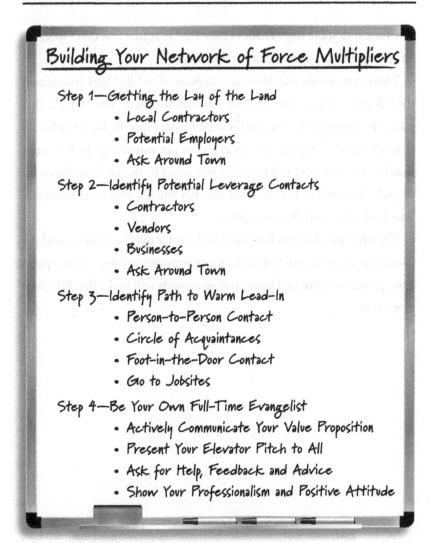

## Building Your Network of Force Multipliers

Step 1—Getting the Lay of the Land
- Local Contractors
- Potential Employers
- Ask Around Town

Step 2—Identify Potential Leverage Contacts
- Contractors
- Vendors
- Businesses
- Ask Around Town

Step 3—Identify Path to Warm Lead-In
- Person-to-Person Contact
- Circle of Acquaintances
- Foot-in-the-Door Contact
- Go to Jobsites

Step 4—Be Your Own Full-Time Evangelist
- Actively Communicate Your Value Proposition
- Present Your Elevator Pitch to All
- Ask for Help, Feedback and Advice
- Show Your Professionalism and Positive Attitude

## THINK LIKE YOUR FUTURE EMPLOYER

Remember, employers want to hire the best possible candidates for their open positions. Put yourself in their shoes. When employers are looking for new employees, they typically have a choice of candidates. You want to position yourself in the best light to ensure that you are THE candidate who gets the job.

Employers want their new employee to not only be willing and equipped with the skills needed to do the job, but to also bring with them the intangibles to add to and succeed with their existing team. These intangibles are the soft skills that are not written into a job description but are nonetheless expected or at least hoped for when an employer is looking to fill positions. Whether you are interviewing or just networking, look for opportunities to let your future employer know that you are a skilled Craftsman and you also have the intangible, soft skills that they are looking for:

- ✓ Solid decision-making skills
- ✓ Ability to learn and take direction
- ✓ Flexibility, adaptability and persistence to get the job done
- ✓ Effective written and verbal communication skills
- ✓ Commitment to delivering an excellent work product every day
- ✓ Work well with others at all levels
- ✓ Professional, ethical, consistent work habits and practices

You want to let your future employer know that you possess those soft skills and you are prepared to commit yourself to succeeding as their new employee.

## DRUG TESTING & GETTING HIRED OR FIRED

A topic that has come up in nearly every interview of successful Subject Matter Experts for this AYB Playbook series is the impact of drug testing on the hiring and firing in the Skilled Trades. As more states in the US pass laws related to drugs, more and more folks are going to get caught up in the long-lasting aftereffects of using drugs.

Many employers require drug testing prior to finalizing a new hire and others conduct random drug testing to ensure that their jobsites are free of drug use, if simply to minimize their legal liabilities. You need to recognize that drug use and drug testing is an important, major factor that will be at play when you are looking to find or keep a job in the Skilled Trades. Enough said.

## WHERE TO TURN FOR MORE INFORMATION

At whatever stage you may be in your career as an HVAC/R Technician, you have a wide array of resources available to help you no matter where you live in the US. Remember: for local resources and opportunities, you should always start with www.CareerOneStop.org to get the ball rolling.

You always have the Web and all the resources that it makes available to you via its search results. However, don't forget that you can always go "old school" and ask for help from your local librarian.

## YOUR LOCAL LIBRARIAN

Whatever you do, do not forget that, even in this age of Google and the Internet, you have a tremendous resource just a few minutes away— waiting, willing and happy to help you jump-start or fine tune your search in whatever you are trying to find. Believe me, do yourself a favor:

- ✓ Go to your local library
- ✓ Walk up to the Information Desk
- ✓ Ask the librarian about whatever you want to explore, then
- ✓ Stand back, watch and see how Google still has some serious competition

## —————— CHAPTER 6 REPLAY ——————
## Finding Work as an HVAC/R Technician

» Your starting point for finding job opportunities in your local market should be www.CareerOneStop.org and the closest American Job Center

» Your full-time job is to find a full-time job. Follow the AYB steps and tools to find a great job:
  • Put together a well-written resume
  • Create your "elevator pitch"
  • Put together your plan of action
  • Take action consistently and don't give up

» Identify your "force multipliers" and start networking with them to leverage their help and connections to others in your search of a great new job

» Think like your future employer. You want to position yourself in the best light to ensure that your prospective employer looks at you as the best candidate for the job

# CHAPTER 7

# At Your Best with 3P+A in Action

# YOU ARE AT YOUR BEST
## *when you are uncompromising in your pursuit of being the best that you can be.*

---

*A price has to be paid for success. Almost invariably those who have reached the summits worked harder and longer, studied and planned more assiduously, practiced more self-denial, overcame more difficulties than those of us who have not risen so far.*

—B. C. FORBES

---

## AT YOUR BEST WITH 3P+A IN ACTION

The formula to ensure success throughout your career is relatively easy and quick to put on paper, but it is definitely difficult and time demanding to execute well. Success comes at a price and there is simply no getting around it with shortcuts or half-measures. Much of what it takes to be successful comes down to common sense, but it does require you to be fully committed to work hard and to stay focused on always creating value for your employer and customers.

Chapter 6 discussed how to find work. This chapter will discuss how to turn the idea of work into your pursuit of a profession where you become a highly valued employee and Craftsman. It will lay out the things that you need to do and think about day in and day out throughout your career to ensure that you succeed at every stage and at every job.

Since the formula for success is not a one-and-done thing, this chapter is intended to provide you a framework of concrete actions and thoughts that you can refer back to over and over again to keep yourself on track. The concepts introduced earlier covering 3P+A will now be expanded to provide you that framework.

- ✓ People
- ✓ Performance
- ✓ Professionalism
- ✓ Attitude

Under each of these four focus areas, you will find a brief discussion of critical topics that you need to internalize and make your own. Do so consistently and you will succeed. Do so and you will become an indispensable, highly valued employee to your employer. I can say this so emphatically because every interview I have had with successful players in the Skilled Trades always comes down to a combination of these traits and mindset as *the* formula for success.

Where appropriate, you will also be directed to specific locations in a great book that I believe could be an invaluable resource for you:

- ✓ *How to Be the Employee Your Company Can't Live Without:*
  *18 Ways to Become Indispensable* by Glenn Shepard

An **AYB Assist** will follow each set of recommended actions with the specific chapter(s) in the Shepard book where you can learn more about a topic without having to read the entire book first. Please know that I do strongly encourage you to read this book through and through and then keep it as a reference. It could become your secret competitive advantage throughout your professional career. With that, let's begin.

## PEOPLE: THE FIRST P IN 3P+A
### Be a Team Player

Theodore Roosevelt said, "The most important single ingredient in the formula of success is knowing how to get along with people." When you are at work, you will nearly always be part of a group—your team. Recognize that your success depends on your contribution to the overall success of your team. Know your place and your responsibilities on your team. Execute the tasks assigned to you to the best of your ability and figure out ways to help others on your team succeed with their tasks without looking for something for yourself in return.

### Know Your Boss

You need to know what your boss's expectations are so that you can set your own expectations and priorities for your work. It is important to ask your boss how and when they prefer communication. The better you understand how your boss thinks and what he or she values, the better that you can perform your job and exceed their expectations.

### Live the Golden Rule

The saying, "Do unto others as you would have them do unto you" covers a lot of ground in how we should interact in life. At work, I believe that it all comes down to respect for others. Be respectful of everyone you come in contact with and you will be respected in return. Even when respect is not given to you, always be known as one who is respectful of everyone—no matter what.

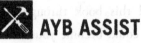

## AYB ASSIST

*How to Be the Employee Your Company Can't Live Without:*
*18 Ways to Become Indispensable*

- Chap. 2: "Learn What Your Boss Wants from You"
- Chap. 10: "Broaden Your Circle of Influence"

## PERFORMANCE: THE SECOND P IN 3P+A
### Be Proactive, Take Initiative

You need to make asking the question, "What can I do to help?" your top-of-mind, go-to thought whenever you have free time while at work. If you want your boss to think of you as a highly valued employee, you must earn that reputation. You do so by always being ready and willing to do more than what was asked of you, looking for opportunities to extend your contribution to your job, your co-workers and your employer. After you've done what you were assigned to do, look for what else needs to be done and do it without having to be asked. Be known for always asking and then following through on "What can I do to help?"

### Be a Problem Solver

Dealing with problems—large and small—in the workplace is a never-ending fact of life. The better you are at solving problems, the more valuable you will become to your employer and your team. Look for opportunities to step up and try to solve problems that arise on the job. Be willing to take on the additional work that solving a problem entails. Do it with a smile on your face and positive, can-do attitude. The ability and willingness to think through an issue that may be hindering or stopping progress on the job to come up with a solution has very real, profit-and-loss implications for your employer. Be known as a problem solver, not as a problem creator or—just as bad—a problem ignorer, who steps back from problems, waiting for someone else to uncover and/or solve them.

## Be That Person That Other People Can Count On— No Matter What

Be reliable. Showing up on time (better yet, a few minutes early), ready to work with the right tools and attitude to hit the ground running every day is a MAJOR differentiating factor that you can own beginning your first day on the job—any job. It is hard to believe that this one simple habit alone can set you apart from the vast majority of your compatriots. It is a matter of respect—for your employer, for your co-workers and for yourself. Strive to be the person on the jobsite who always is ready to "step up" whenever things get tough or an extra hand is needed to accomplish a task. No matter what, be known for being reliable.

## Take Pride in Your Competence

There is a big difference between doing your job and doing your job well. Activity for activity's sake is not doing your job well. Experience the phenomenal feeling of completing a job well done. Make it a habit. Let your competence become an obsession. It will serve you many times over throughout your entire career. Earn the reputation for always doing your job accurately and thoroughly. Be known for always doing your best work even when no one is looking.

## AYB ASSIST

*How to Be the Employee Your Company Can't Live Without:*
*18 Ways to Become Indispensable*

- Chap. 8: "Become the Most Reliable Person in Your Company"
- Chap. 12: "Be a Professional in Whatever You Do"
- Chap. 17: "Become a Problem Solver"

## PROFESSIONALISM: THE THIRD P IN 3P+A
### Create Value in All that You Do—All Day, Every Day

You've probably heard the saying: "Nothing personal. It's just business." Well, the bottom line—literally—is that every business must make a profit to survive. On the most basic level, your overall value to your employer comes down to how much of the work you do contributes to the profitability of the business. This is a reality of life in business. Nothing personal.

Knowing this, look at everything you do while you are on the job. Ask yourself, "Am I creating value for my employer with what I am doing right now?" Then ask yourself, "If 'time is money' and my employer needs to make a profit to pay my salary, am I wasting time and money by what I am doing or not doing?"

Always be looking for ways to create value in everything you do. Be known for never wasting your employer's time and money.

### Take Responsibility, No Excuses

Things happen. Mistakes happen. Taking initiative, pushing to accomplish more and learning new things involve the risk of setbacks. When they do happen, take immediate responsibility. No excuses. Point it out to your boss if needed. Don't hide it. Apologize and assure your boss that it will not happen again. Then, resolve to learn from the issue and not repeat it. Be known for always being a person of character, who is the first to stand up to your mistakes and wherever possible provide the fix.

### Be Known for No Drama, No Special Treatment and Low Maintenance

The workplace functions best when there is no drama brewing from personal issues or having to accommodate peculiarities of an individual over the rest of a team or having to deal with the demands from a high-maintenance individual. Your employer has no choice but to get rid of anyone who impacts the team negatively too much or often.

- ✓ Be known for being no drama: Leave your problems and issues at home. Everyone has their own problems at home. Avoid gossip. Avoid people who gossip or create drama
- ✓ Be known for needing no special treatment: Don't cherry-pick the easier projects. Put your phone on silent and forget it's in your pocket until you're either on break or off for the day. Do whatever needs to be done and do it with a smile on your face
- ✓ Be known for being low maintenance: Your boss has a lot to think about every day. Avoid people and activities that end up requiring your boss's attention beyond those needed to get the work done. Don't give your employer the reason to put you on the "first-to-go" list

## ⚒ AYB ASSIST

*How to Be the Employee Your Company Can't Live Without: 18 Ways to Become Indispensable*
- Chap. 3: "Be Low Maintenance"

- Chap. 5: "Understanding the Economic Realities of Employing People"
- Chap. 9: "Learn the Right Way to Make Mistakes"
- Chap. 12 "Be Professional at Whatever You Do"

## ATTITUDE: THE A IN 3P+A
### Always Be a Can-Do Person

As the saying goes, "Where there's a will, there's a way." Commit yourself to always having the will to "get it done." Never quit. Just get it done. Don't look at obstacles as reasons to be like everyone else, who stop pursuing their objectives or finishing a task because it gets difficult. Take on each of the obstacles as a way to differentiate yourself from the rest. Be known for always doing whatever it takes to reach your goal and get it done.

### Execute Like This Is Your Dream Job—No Matter What

Whatever job you have at any given time, remember that it is your choice to be there. You are accepting a paycheck from your employer in exchange for the services that you agreed to deliver. Even if the job doesn't really interest you, as long as you hold the position, go into work acting like this job is the realization of your life-long passion.

Giving 100 percent at your job—whatever your job may be—becomes a habit if you choose to make it habit. Make it a habit. If you give 100 percent at a job that doesn't interest you, then just imagine how you will be when you have the job you really dream about. The added benefit is that if, along the way, you ask your boss, "What can I do to EARN that position?" he/she will be more likely to believe that you can deliver. You've already showed your character and attitude.

### *Leave Your Ego Behind*

You have *a lot* to learn and many years of experience to acquire in order to legitimately consider yourself a Craftsman. Accept it. Embrace it. Be humble but be confident that you can make it happen. Take criticism and guidance gracefully. Seek out mentors to "show you the ropes." Whatever stage you may be in your career, many others have been exactly where you find yourself with the same questions and insecurities. Ask questions if you aren't sure of how to do something. You will be surprised how helpful your co-workers will be if you are eager to learn from them. Take advantage of the expertise that they have, and you need. Someday you can be in the position to pay it forward to help the next generation of people like you. Be known for being more concerned about learning how to do it right than worrying about who gets the credit or about how it might make you look.

 **AYB ASSIST**

*How to Be the Employee Your Company Can't Live Without:*
*18 Ways to Become Indispensable*

- Chap. 6: "Act Like You Own the Place"
- Chap. 14: "Take Charge of Your Own Destiny"
- Chap. 16: "Avoid Learned Helplessness"

—————— **CHAPTER 7 REPLAY** ——————
#### At Your Best with 3P+A in Action

» People: The First P in 3P+A
- Be a team player
- Know your boss
- Live the Golden Rule

» Performance: The Second P in 3P+A
  • Be proactive, take initiative
  • Be a problem solver
  • Be a person that other people can count on—no matter what
  • Take pride in your competence
» Professionalism: The Third P in 3P+A
  • Create value in all that you do—all day, every day
  • Take responsibility, no excuses
  • Be known for no drama, no special treatment and low maintenance
» Attitude: The A in 3P+A
  • Always be a can-do person
  • Execute like *this* is your dream job—no matter what
  • Leave your ego behind

# CHAPTER 8

# Getting Your Head Straight, Part 1

# Getting Your Head Straight, Part 1

# YOU ARE AT YOUR BEST
## *when you can get your head straight,*
## *especially when the going gets tough.*

---

## GETTING YOUR HEAD STRAIGHT, PART 1

Professional athletes look to their coaches and trainers to help them be at their best. In order to be successful at anything, you, too, need to be **At Your Best**. However, you don't always have a coach or trainer to keep you on track working on your career objectives. For better or worse, it is up to you to "get your head straight" when the inevitable self-doubt and second guessing your life choices creeps into your thinking.

To be **At Your Best**, it takes daily commitment and focus to get up every morning and push yourself to become the Craftsman that you know you want to become. You also need to accept that it is up to you and only you to get yourself back on track. Getting your head straight by changing what you are focusing on is one way for you to redirect your thinking from self-doubt to belief in yourself; from second guessing your decisions to recommitting yourself to their realization.

The critically important thing to remember about getting your head straight is that you can do it anytime or anywhere. You are in control. You simply have to decide that you have had enough of the self-doubt, the second guessing, the negative thoughts and the bad attitude and that you need to replace them with new, better, positive thoughts that support your intentions.

These new, better, affirming thoughts—**attitude adjusters**—can either be those that you have come up with on your own, or they can be thoughts offered up by others who have overcome hurdles in their own lives. In the section following this discussion, you will find a number of attitude adjusters—insights and motivational quotes from some notable folks—that you might consider. Look them over and find those that resonate with you.

Then, when you feel like you need to get your head straight, do the following:

✓ Read these attitude adjusters—out loud or to yourself; the same one multiple times or one after another. Your choice
✓ Think about how they apply to your immediate situation and internalize that feeling
✓ Consider how your situation would improve if you could live/act according to the alternative viewpoint
✓ Commit yourself to shifting your thinking from the negative to the positive
✓ Then, get on with life. Get back to work. Get back to moving toward your objectives
  • Just know and accept that this is not a "one-and-done" thing. When negative thinking creeps in, be armed and ready to fight it with better alternatives and positive attitude adjustment. Get into the habit of actively attacking thoughts of self-doubt and second guessing before they can take control of your day or your life

**Remember:** Only you can control your attitude—every day, all day.

If you have come up with your own list of attitude adjusters, something that you heard or came up with on your own, great! List them out so that you have easy, ready access to them whenever you need them.

- ✓ Write them out in a "go-to" list on a piece of paper and put it in your wallet or your glove compartment or your tool box or wherever works for you. (By the way, you might want to laminate it, if you take this route)
- ✓ Type out your go-to list into the "Notes" app on your smartphone so you can refer to them while everyone else is checking their email and social media posts
- ✓ Write them out on another piece of paper and tape it to your mirror so you can see it every morning and evening. For example:
  1. Listen More
  2. Interrupt Less
  3. Ask More Questions

If you would rather consider the perspectives of other notable people who have overcome challenges, that, too, is great! Consider the quotes presented in the rest of this section. Pick a few—as many of the ones that hit you head-on when you read them—and put them on your go-to list or smartphone.

**AYB Quick Tool:** Go to www.AtYourBest.com and click on "**AYB Quick Tools.**" You will find a link to **Getting Your Head Straight.** All the quotes are grouped according to their focus and then categorized under one of four headings: People, Performance, Professionalism & Attitude, or 3P+A. The comments provided by the SMEs are presented under those categories as "SME Insights."

Now, read through the following insights and quotes and take a moment to pick the two in each group that resonate with you or impact you when you first read them. Then, put a check mark in the space next to it. Your objective is to find a couple attitude adjusters in each of the 3P+A categories that you can quickly refer back to when things get difficult.

## PEOPLE:

### SME Insights about People:

*Be teachable and be humble.*
                              —STEVE M., CONTRACTOR, NEW YORK

*Prove yourself to be responsible and reliable. Accept and own up to your mistakes. Man up! You'll be 90 to 95 percent further ahead of your competition.*
                              —JERRY K., CONTRACTOR, KANSAS

*Learning communication skills is critical to how far you can go. You need to know how to communicate with your boss or your customer or you are dead in the water.*
                              —GARTH B., CONTRACTOR, ATLANTA

## Quotes to Get Your Head Straight about People:

*People who are unable to motivate themselves must be content with mediocrity, no matter how impressive their other talents.*

—ANDREW CARNEGIE

*Not everyone thinks the way you think, knows the things you know, believes the things you believe, nor acts the way that you would act. Remember this and you will go a long way in getting along with people.*

—ARTHUR FORMAN

*Keep away from people who belittle your ambitions. Small people always do that, but the really great make you feel that you, too, can become great.*

—MARK TWAIN

*Any fool can criticize, complain and condemn—and most fools do. But it takes character and self-control to be understanding and forgiving.*

—DALE CARNEGIE

*The measure of a man's character is what he would do if he knew he would never be found out.*

—THOMAS MACAULAY

*People with good intentions make promises. People with good character keep them.*

—UNKNOWN

*Anyone who waits for someone else to make a change automatically becomes a follower.*

—PEYTON MANNING

*People don't care how much you know until they know how you care.*

—THEODORE ROOSEVELT

*Most people fail in life not because they aim too high and miss, but because they aim too low and hit.*

—LES BROWN

*Most people fail because they major in the minor things.*

—ANTHONY ROBBINS

## PERFORMANCE:

### *SME Insights about Performance:*

---

*Don't over-complicate the simple stuff. Don't over-simplify the complicated stuff.*

—JEREMY H., CONTRACTOR, SEATTLE AREA

*Clean up your mess without having to be asked. Take initiative. Just get it done and don't look for somebody to pat you on your back. It's your job.*

—JERRY M., CONTRACTOR, ST. LOUIS

*Ask questions if you're not 100 percent sure about what you're doing or being asked to do. Don't just assume that you can figure it out along the way. Don't be afraid or embarrassed to ask questions, It's OK. Everyone ahead of you was there before you.*

—AL P., CONTRACTOR, NEW YORK

---

### *Quotes to Get Your Head Straight about Performance:*

---

*Performance is the best way to shut people up.*

—MARCUS LEMONIS

*There are no traffic jams in the extra mile.*

—ROGER STAUBACH

*Nothing will work unless you do.*

—JOHN WOODEN

*There are no secrets to success. It is the result of preparation, hard work and learning from failure.*

—COLIN POWELL

*Shortcuts lead to long delays.*

—MIKE ROWE

*Whatever your life's work is, do it well. A man should do his job so well that the living, the dead and the unborn could do it no better.*

—MARTIN LUTHER KING, JR.

*Be so good they can't ignore you.*

—STEVE MARTIN

*I've always believed that if you put in the work, the results will come. I don't do things half-heartedly. Because if I do, then I can expect half-hearted results.*

—MICHAEL JORDAN

*Performance, and performance alone, dictates the apex predator in any food chain.*

—US NAVY SEAL SAYING

*High performance, high reward. Low performance, there's the door.*

—MARCUS LEMONIS

## PROFESSIONALISM:

### *SME Insights about Professionalism:*

*Dress like a professional. This isn't some fashion show for non-conformists trying to make a statement. This is a place of work. Respect the profession. Respect your co-workers. Respect yourself. Respect your employer and the customer. They are paying your salary.*

—BRIAN M., CONTRACTOR, SEATTLE AREA

*Always show up with the required tools to do the job. If you're always asking people for their tools, you are going to have real problems being successful.*

—KEN C., CONTRACTOR, SEATTLE AREA

*Two ears and one mouth. Two to one—that should be the minimum ratio between your time listening versus your time talking. Bottom line: shut up and do the work.*

—ALEJANDRO M., CONTRACTOR, NEW YORK

*Stay off your cell phone. You're wasting somebody else's money.*

—HARRY S., CONTRACTOR, NEW YORK

## Quotes to Get Your Head Straight about Professionalism:

*A professional is someone who does his best work when he doesn't feel like it.*

—ALISTAIR COOKE

*When your work speaks for itself, don't interrupt.*

—HENRY J. KAISER

*Live in such a way that if someone spoke badly about you, no one would believe it.*

—UNKNOWN


*Nobody who ever gave his best regretted it.*

—GEORGE S. HALAS


*You did not wake up today to be mediocre.*

—UNKNOWN

*There are no limitations to the minds except those that we acknowledge.*

—NAPOLEON HILL


*Nothing worth having comes easy.*

—THEODORE ROOSEVELT


*Always do more than is required of you.*

—GENERAL GEORGE PATTON


*There are no shortcuts to anyplace worthwhile.*

—BEVERLY SILLS

*The elevator to success is out of order. You'll have to use the stairs . . . one at a time.*

—JOE GIRARD

## ATTITUDE:

### *SME Insights about Attitude:*

*You're going to work with lots of angry, unpleasant, opinionated people in your career. That's the way it is. That's life. Work still needs to get done. There is no place for your bad attitude or your mouth.*

—ERNIE M. CONTRACTOR, SEATTLE AREA

*Having a great attitude is the most important thing. Attitude is more important than your schooling, your birth country or if you have only a nickel in your pocket. With a good attitude you can make anything happen for you and your family in this country. If your attitude is bad, I want nothing to do with you and no one else will either . . . maybe your mother.*

—IVAN P., CONTRACTOR, NEW YORK

*Put in 100 percent, 100 percent of the time.*

—GARTH B., CONTRACTOR, ATLANTA

## Quotes to Get Your Head Straight about Attitude:

*There can be no positive result through a negative attitude. Think positive. Live positive.*

—ALBERT EINSTEIN

*A bad attitude is like a flat tire. If you don't change it, you'll go nowhere.*

—JOHN N. MITCHELL

*Attitude is more important than the past, than education, than money, than circumstances, than what people say. It is more important than appearance, giftedness or skill.*

—CHARLES SWINDOLL

*Your attitude is like a price tag. It shows how valuable you are.*

—UNKNOWN

*We would accomplish many more things if we did not think them as impossible.*

—VINCE LOMBARDI

*Be humble. Be hungry. And always be the hardest worker in the room.*

—UNKNOWN

*The greatest discovery of all time is that a person can change his future by merely changing his attitude.*

—OPRAH WINFREY

*The problem is not the problem. The problem is your attitude about the problem. Do you understand?*

—CAPTAIN JACK SPARROW

*Life is 10 percent what happens to you, and 90 percent how you respond to it.*

—LOU HOLTZ

*Never, never, never give up.*

—WINSTON CHURCHILL

---

## ——— CHAPTER 8 REPLAY ———
### Getting Your Head Straight, Part 1

» The best world-class athletes have coaches and trainers to help them keep at their best. Let the quotes and insights listed above help you "get your head straight."

  • Replace self-doubt and negativity with new empowering, positive thoughts

» When necessary, do the following:
  • Read through the insights and quotes
  • Select the two in each group that resonates with you
  • Write them down and post them where you can see them often
  • Then, hitch up your pants and get back to work
» Only you can control your attitude—all day, every day

# PART 3:

# At Your Best as a Small Business: Building a World-Class Franchise

You have built up your skills and experience to the point to where you now believe that you can be successful by offering your services as a self-employed, small business owner. Chances are very good that you are right. The demand for high-quality service providers in the Skilled Trades has never been higher and that demand will only continue to grow well into the future.

Part 3 of this AYB Playbook will focus on the critical success factors that you should consider maximizing your potential to be **At Your Best** as a small business. In keeping with the idea of this being a Playbook or your game plan for success, we are going expand on the sports analogy for the balance of this AYB Playbook. Part 3 is divided into five sections:

**AYB: Pre-Game**

✓ What you need to consider and do before you strike out on your own, along with an important tool for future use in your business planning

## AYB: Kick Off

✓ What you need to have in place at the point that you launch your self-employed, small business

## AYB: Game On

✓ What you need to focus on day in and day out as a successful small business—beyond the work at hand

## AYB: Halftime

✓ What you need to regularly review, reassess and readjust to ensure that you stay on the path to success

## AYB: Going Pro

✓ What you need to consider in order to grow your small business to the "next level"

## AYB PLAYBOOKS & RECOMMENDED READING

Starting and running a successful small business can be extremely difficult—and, even that may be an understatement. Every day across the US, countless small businesses die painful deaths and their owners suffer the financial and emotional consequences. However, working together, we are going to make sure that this does not happen to You, Inc.

The reasons for small business failures usually come down to some predictable, critical success factors that were missed. These critical success factors can be categorized as follows:

✓ Consistent Delivery of High Quality Service
✓ Focus on Customer Service and Loyalty
✓ Financial and Cashflow Management

- ✓ Effectiveness of Business Operation and Processes
- ✓ Success in Sales and Marketing
- ✓ Small Team Leadership

Failing at any one of these critical success factors does not guarantee failure of You, Inc. However, each of these factors, in and of themselves can kill your business. If a small business is not executing on two or more of these factors at the same time, the odds of going out of business grows exponentially until the weight of the issues kill the business—but not You, Inc., because you will be forewarned and prepared.

- ✓ If the quality of You, Inc.'s services is inconsistent, your reputation will suffer
- ✓ If You, Inc.'s customer service is lacking, and your customers are not loyal, you will not see repeat business
- ✓ If You, Inc.'s financials are not kept in order, you will run into money problems—guaranteed
- ✓ If You, Inc.'s paperwork and other back-office operations are not organized, you will be frustrated at best or, at worst, you will run into serious legal, financial and/or tax problems
- ✓ If You, Inc.'s efforts to generate business for itself is passive or substandard, you will only see little or no revenue growth
- ✓ If You, Inc.'s team is limited by your ability to lead, you will also limit your overall growth and your ability to attract other high-quality craftsmen

The overarching objective of this AYB Playbook is to give you a "look beyond the horizon" to arm you with the right questions to ask and the right issues to think about as you build You, Inc. Given that you are now considering striking out on your own, you are going to have to learn and master an entirely new set of skills to meet the challenge of these "predictable, critical success factors."

Part 3 of this AYB Playbook will discuss these "critical success factors" at a high level to cover what you need to consider. In order to get a more in depth understanding of these topics, you will be directed to five books that present their position on those topics in much more detail. There is no doubt that there are any number of books and resources that you can use to learn more about any business subject that you can imagine. I strongly encourage you to do so.

However, in an effort to give you a starting point, as well as to narrow the scope of what you need to read on a particular subject, I will suggest specific sections or chapters in one or more of five books covering five main focus areas.

The books that I will reference in the coming pages and that I strongly recommend that you purchase are:

### *Small Time Operator*, 13th edition by Bernard Kamaroff

This book offers a clear, straightforward explanation of each important back office element and decision faced by a small business, including issues related to finances, legal, tax, insurance, employees and much more. Although the other books noted below are important, I suggest that you make *Small Time Operator* your constant companion and guide to help yourself avoid the BIG mistakes in operating a small business.

### *The Art of the Start* by Guy Kawasaki

This book provides an innovative look at how to approach launching You, Inc., including how to build your Go-To-Market Plan.

*Raving Fans: A Revolutionary Approach to Customer Service*
by Ken Blanchard & Sheldon Bowles

This book will change your perspective on delivering excellent customer service for the better, making it customer service You, Inc.'s unbeatable competitive advantage.

*Guerrilla Marketing Remix* by Jay Conrad Levinson & Jeannie Levinson

This book is a compilation of short presentations of guerrilla marketing and other guerrilla business strategies that you can employ to build You, Inc. "Guerrilla" business strategies leverage your imagination, energy and time to help you aggressively promote your products or services in unconventional ways. These strategies are specifically designed for small businesses with few resources and limited budgets.

*Extreme Ownership: How U.S. Navy SEALS Lead and Win* by Jocko Willink & Leif Babin

This book is all about leading and motivating a small team of highly trained folks to work effectively to realize a common goal.

## THE NEED FOR SOME BACK-UP

There is a great deal of important, new information that you need to master in order to be successful in launching and growing a small business in the Skilled Trades. No one book can do justice to this objective—especially this AYB Playbook given that it is intended to be a brief, direct action plan. That is the reason for these other books.

My recommendation is that you go online and order your copies of these five books. It is your choice as to whether you wait to continue reading this AYB Playbook now or wait until you have the other books to refer to while you read. Either way, you will have an **AYB Assist** at the end of key sections that direct you to specific sections or chapters in these books to quickly learn more about a subject without having to read the entire book.

It is up to you. Do you read this Playbook first and then use **AYB Assists** to highlight key sections when you read the recommended books? Or, do you read this Playbook and while you read Part 3, you use the **AYB Assists** to expand your understanding of a topic in real time? You choose, but my recommendation is that you have your copy of each book available while you read Part 3. The information is too important and necessary for the success of You, Inc. My bottom line objective is to give you a quick reference, so you can further your understanding of particular topics by learning about from world-class, Subject Matter Experts.

To be **At Your Best**, you will need to do the hard work of learning new skills and gain new knowledge to become successful. You cannot leave it to chance. You need a plan and you need to work your plan. Along the way, you need to take advantage of those who have come before you and get them to coach you on how best to do things. Make these books part of your team of "success coaches."

# CHAPTER 9

# At Your Best:
# The Pre-Game

# YOU ARE AT YOUR BEST
### *when you have a plan—before you strike out on your own.*

---

## AT YOUR BEST BEFORE THE GAME

For the purpose of the rest of this Playbook, we will assume that you have developed yourself as a Craftsman on a solid foundation of skills, knowledge and experience with a commitment to being **At Your Best** by focusing on your best efforts and attitude: your 3P+A (People, Performance, Professionalism & Attitude).

We can now move on to what you need to consider if you are going to launch a successful, small business. This is definitely one of those Kitchen Table Moments, if you hadn't noticed. You have to admit, it is exciting to think about being your own boss!

As daunting the prospect of striking out on your own might be, please know that given the rock-solid foundation that you have built to be **At Your Best**, you do have what it takes to be successful. Still, before you actually launch, you want to be able to answer and/or take action on the following types of questions:

✓ What are the risks of launching your small business, You, Inc., and are you prepared to deal with them? Financial risks? Personal relationship risks? Career risks?

✓ How much uncertainty is too much for you? How will you handle the uncertainty regarding giving up your regular paycheck? How will you handle the uncertainty about being able to find new business opportunities for You, Inc.?

✓ What would the impact of either success or failure be on you, your family or those important to you?

✓ What are the trade-offs that you are going to have to make and are you prepared to make them?

✓ How will your important personal relationships be impacted or possibly jeopardized by launching You, Inc.? Less time with your family?

✓ How much have you saved up to protect your downside, while you launch You, Inc.?

✓ It may take 12–18 months before you can earn what you are currently earning. Can you handle that? How much of a financial backstop or buffer have you built?

✓ Are you prepared to invest all your available time to making You, Inc. successful? Is that enough?

## YOU, INC. AS A SMALL BUSINESS

In Part 1 of this AYB Playbook, we referred to you and You, Inc. as the same individual—an employee. You, Inc. was in the business of selling your time and services to your employer, for which you were paid a wage. In Part 3, we will use You, Inc. to refer to you as a small business selling your firm's services to your customers, for which you will invoice them and they will pay your company.

You and You, Inc. need to do a great deal of thinking and planning in order to give yourself the best chance for long-term business success. There are many topics to consider along the way and there are no short-cuts. It must be done and you are the one to do it. Let's get started but first, you will need a useful tool that we will come back to over and over—the **SWOT Analysis**.

---

*Successful people ask better questions, and as a result, they get better answers.*

—ANTHONY ROBBINS

---

## SWOT EARLY & OFTEN

Deciding to strike out on your own is definitely a daunting "Kitchen Table Moment" if there ever was one. In order to do so effectively, you want to make sure that you have considered the pros and cons of the many decisions you will need to make—as completely and as objectively as you can. One tool or approach that works extraordinarily well to get yourself to think through those pros and cons in a structured manner is called a SWOT analysis.

**SWOT** stands for:
- **S:** Strengths
- **W:** Weaknesses
- **O:** Opportunities
- **T:** Threats

Try to always choose a specific purpose for your SWOT analysis. By being specific about what you are trying to analyze, you can avoid coming up with generalizations that may not translate well into an action plan. Don't try to do an all-encompassing SWOT analysis on everything all at once. Spread it out. In other words, select something specific to analyze like: Should You, Inc. enter a particular line of business at this time? versus What type of business should You, Inc. become? Whereas analyzing the first question will result in specific answers, the second will result a lot of generalities that will not be as helpful.

You can do a SWOT analysis on nearly any business decision/situation that you might encounter to flesh out the positive and the negative sides of a business issue you face. That is why this section is called "SWOT Early & Often." Even doing a SWOT analysis on the back of a napkin can bring clarity to an important decision or issue, if that is all you have in front of you.

The first two categories of issues (Strengths and Weaknesses) refer to internal factors affecting the potential outcome of a business decision/issue. The second two (Opportunities and Threats) refer to external factors impacting the potential outcome.

You can do a SWOT analysis on one page in a four-quadrant box such as shown opposite or on four different pages, one page for each category or on a whiteboard or on whatever works best for you. The important thing is to be brutally objective and complete. List out all the issues and call-outs you can think of in each category in order to give yourself a clearer picture for all the critical elements of the decision/issue you face.

## SWOT Analysis

| STRENGTHS | WEAKNESSES |
|---|---|
| ✓ What elements of this decision/issue give You, Inc. an **advantage** over other approaches that you could take?<br>✓ What are your **positive** differentiators that favor you or your offering over the competition?<br>✓ What resources and/or skills do you have that set you apart? | ✓ What elements of this decision or issue give it a **disadvantage** over other approaches?<br>✓ What are your **negative** differentiators that favor your competition over you?<br>✓ What resources and/or skills are you missing? |
| OPPORTUNITIES | THREATS |
| ✓ What are the elements of the local market or the competitive landscape that could be exploited or leveraged to work to your **advantage**?<br>✓ What customer(s), event(s) or economic conditions make it **favorable** for the decision to go forward? | ✓ What are the elements of the local market or the competitive landscape that could cause problems or be detrimental and work to your **disadvantage**?<br>✓ What customer(s), event(s) or economic conditions make it **unfavorable** for the decision to go forward? |

**AYB Quick Tool:** Go to www.AtYourBest.com and click on "**AYB Quick Tools**" for a sample, Microsoft Word–based **SWOT Analysis** worksheet that you can download and easily modify for your purposes.

## LAUNCH YOU, INC. WITH YOUR EYES WIDE OPEN

Everyone is different. Everyone has a different tolerance for risk. Everyone has different needs and wants in their lives. Therefore, there can be no "one-size-fits-all" approach to determining whether you are in the right place and time to launch a new small business. Just remember, given the rock-solid foundation that you have built to be **At Your Best**, you do have what it takes to be successful. However, the questions you need to ask yourself to come down to some version of:

- ✓ Why do I want to do it?
- ✓ What will it cost me?
- ✓ What will I have to give up?
- ✓ What am I putting at risk?
- ✓ How will I know when the right time is?

After you have asked yourself—and answered—these questions, you want to follow up with answering:

- ✓ What are the potential benefits/upsides to launching You, Inc.?
- ✓ Why do I want to run my own small business?

Finally, you need to ask yourself:

- ✓ Given your answers, is it worth it to launch You, Inc. now, later or not at all?

You really want to devote your time and focus—beforehand—to consider whether it is the right time for you to launch your small business. Once you are in the "thick of things," you will not have a lot of time to second-guess yourself. It is better to think through your options and act to minimize any negative impacts prior to having to make your all-out commitment to the new You, Inc.

Take a few minutes to jot down some of your thoughts and answers to the questions that come to you at this point.

### You, Inc.'s First SWOT Analysis

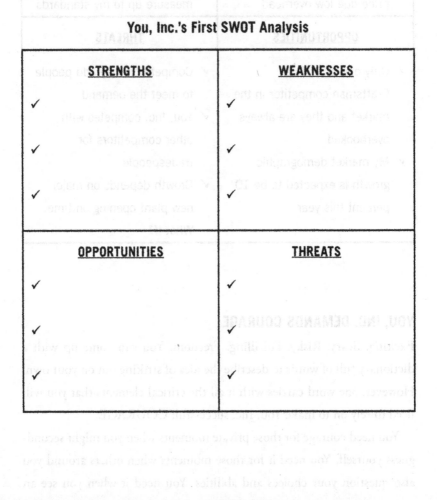

| STRENGTHS | WEAKNESSES |
|---|---|
| ✓ | ✓ |
| ✓ | ✓ |
| ✓ | ✓ |
| **OPPORTUNITIES** | **THREATS** |
| ✓ | ✓ |
| ✓ | ✓ |
| ✓ | ✓ |

Given that this is your first real go-around, here is a quick example of a SWOT Analysis for a contractor considering expanding his/her business with just a few of the things that could be important to consider:

| STRENGTHS | WEAKNESSES |
|---|---|
| ✓ Reputation for quality work<br>✓ Can be super competitive on price due low overhead | ✓ Fine quality takes time<br>✓ Hard to find tradespeople to measure up to my standards |
| OPPORTUNITIES | THREATS |
| ✓ Only one other fine Craftsman competitor in the market and they are always overbooked<br>✓ My market demographic growth is expected to be 10 percent this year | ✓ Competition may add people to meet the demand<br>✓ You, Inc. competes with other competitors for tradespeople<br>✓ Growth depends on major new plant opening on time. What if? |

## YOU, INC. DEMANDS COURAGE

Exciting. Scary. Risky. Fulfilling. Freedom. You can come up with a dictionary full of words to describe the idea of striking out on your own. However, one word carries with it all the critical elements that you will need to rely on to make You, Inc. successful: COURAGE.

You need courage for those private moments when you might second-guess yourself. You need it for those moments when others around you also question your choices and abilities. You need it when you see an opportunity clearly that no one else sees. You must have courage for those moments when things may not go your way. You need to have courage:

- ✓ To do the right thing every time
- ✓ To meet challenges head-on with a positive, can-do attitude
- ✓ To seek out and not be concerned about the uncomfortable and the unknown
- ✓ To believe in yourself even when others do not
- ✓ To lead and help others when you are still learning yourself
- ✓ To risk being embarrassed but to know that since it is worth doing so it must be done
- ✓ To have anxiety and work through it
- ✓ To ask other people for help even when it makes you feel uncomfortable
- ✓ To seek advice from those who may know more or be more successful

We all have great days and not so great days. The reality is that some days you are "on" and some days you're not. On those days when you are not **At Your Best**, get to work. Do something positive for yourself, for your family or for your business. Nothing works better to get you out of a "funk" than getting to work. Focus your mind on all the challenges you've already overcome to build You, Inc. Count your blessings. Know that tomorrow, you will be fired up again—but you simply cannot allow yourself to waste today. Again, count your blessings and that will help you through the tough days. Commit to being **At Your Best**.

*With curiosity comes learning and new ideas. If you are not doing that, you're going to have a real problem.*

—MICHAEL DELL

## YOU, INC. DEMANDS CURIOSITY

No one has all the answers. Success comes to those who know what questions to ask to discover innovative approaches to issues that arise. To be successful as a small business, you should always be curious about:

✓ Your competition
  • What are they doing well that you could incorporate into your business?
  • How is your industry serving the customer's needs?
✓ Your customer
  • What makes them respond positively versus negatively?
  • How can you add value to their experience?
✓ Your city and town around you
  • What is happening in the economics and demographics that will impact your business?
  • How can you take advantage of median income or population growth?
✓ Your fellow team members
  • What motivates them?
  • How can you help improve their motivation?
✓ New ways to solve problems and fix issues
  • What's causing problems and why?
  • How can you change processes to improve outcome?

✓ What's happening in politics and economics in the world
  • How will that impact your business?
  • What can a broader perspective and diverse exposure help you learn?

## MAKE THE WEB YOUR BUSINESS PARTNER

One final point before the Kick Off. You need to make the Web your partner in building a successful You, Inc. Supplement what you read in this AYB Playbook and on the www.AtYouBest.com site with what the Web has to offer—for free.

Earlier in this AYB Playbook, we discussed the value of making YouTube and other online video sites your best friends in learning more about any topic. We discussed how all you have to do is go to www.YouTube.com and click on the magnifying glass icon. The search field will come up and then just let your imagination run wild.

From seasoned craftsmen in the trades to neophytes, and every level in between, folks have uploaded videos presenting their perspectives on how to accomplish something specific or on ways to think through a process you may have encountered. You can also check out the additional information available on other video and how-to sites like: Vimeo, WikiHow, eHow and Instructables. However, these are not the only type of free instructional videos you can find on the Web.

The Web also gives you access to some incredibly valuable business training courses that are free and designed to help you build You, Inc. into the strong, thriving small business that you want. There are a number of courseware sites that you can visit, but I recommend that you at least consider the following two to help you further your education and understanding of business.

## SMALL BUSINESS ADMINISTRATION'S LEARNING CENTER

The Small Business Administration (SBA) is a tremendous resource for you in many ways. It is the US Government agency chartered to support entrepreneurs and small businesses like You, Inc. I will leave it to you to explore the other ways that the SBA might be able to help You, Inc. beyond its business training courses.

The SBA has an excellent selection of business training courses available for free and accessible to you whenever you want via their Learning Center. Just go to: www.sba.gov/learning-center and browse through their wide array of courses on planning, launching and managing your small business. Each session is easy to follow and only take about thirty minutes to complete.

## MY OWN BUSINESS, INC.

My Own Business, Inc. (MOBI) is a nonprofit organization associated with Santa Clara University. MOBI offers an excellent and free, online business training program that is divided into two elements: "Starting a Business" and "Business Expansion." Each of these elements is composed of fifteen sessions. I believe that the sessions encompassing "Starting a Business" would be extremely valuable to you and You, Inc.

Go to www.scu.edu/mobi and click "Our Programs." On the resulting webpage, click on "Starting a Business" and you will see a breakdown of the fifteen sessions. I truly believe that the information provided in these fifteen sessions will be critical to your success in growing You, Inc.

---

## CHAPTER 9 REPLAY
### At Your Best: The Pre-Game

» Launching You, Inc. to become a successful small business must first start with detailed planning and answering some important questions, such as:
  * What are the risks inherent in launching your small business and are you prepared to deal with them?
  * How much uncertainty is too much for you and are you prepared to deal with it?
  * How much have you saved up to support your business launch and to protect your downside?
» Use a SWOT analysis to help you review the pros and cons of decisions that you will need to make in your business planning
  * S is for the Strengths internal, within or inherent in You, Inc. related to the issue
  * W is for Weaknesses internal, within or inherent in You, Inc. related to the issue
  * O is for Opportunities external, outside of You, Inc. but affecting the issue
  * T is for Threats external, outside of You, Inc. but affecting the issue
» Make the Web your business partner. Take advantage of free but invaluable online resources as you do your strategic planning
  * www.AtYourBest.com
  * Small Business Administration's Learning Center—www.sba.gov/learning-center
  * My Own Business, Inc. (MOBI)—www.scu.edu/mobi

# CHAPTER 10

# At Your Best:
# The Kick Off

# At Your Best:
# The Kick Off

## You, Inc. will be
# AT YOUR BEST
## with a solid foundation.

---

## AT YOUR BEST FROM THE START

You have made the decision to be your own boss. You know that you have the skills and experience to be successful as long as you have the fundamentals in place for starting your business.

Putting these critical elements in place to support your efforts to launch a successful small business takes thought and planning. There is no magic or secret shortcut to doing what needs to be done. It comes down to doing the work just as diligently as you would every day in your craft.

The work to be done requires you to ask yourself a great many, substantive questions and then answer them. A straightforward way to think through the wide array of topics and issues in front of you, is to list out your questions in six categories: What, Why, Who, How, When and Where.

It doesn't matter if you do it all over a long weekend or if you do it as a year-long process. It doesn't matter if you do it in a single, comprehensive document or on all sorts of loose sheets of paper. It doesn't even matter if you get your questions on paper but end up leaving some unanswered. What does matter is that you have thought through what it will take to launch You, Inc.—your small business.

Later in this section, we use some of these questions for some important planning exercises. Try to be as comprehensive as you can to exhaust the possibilities so at the end you know you have at least considered what may come up in the future. For example, here is a possible starting point to spark your imagination and add your own questions:

"What" questions:
- ✓ What is a realistic Sales Forecast for You, Inc.?
- ✓ What is your initial Expense Budget? What makes up your budget?
- ✓ What kind of back-office setup and support do you need in place before you launch?
- ✓ What are You, Inc.'s specific service offering(s) and specific competitive advantage(s)?
- ✓ What will you do to stand apart from the competition?
- ✓ What can you offer that no other competitor does?
- ✓ What . . . _____
- ✓ What . . . _____
- ✓ What . . . _____

"Why" questions:
- ✓ Why is now the time right to launch You, Inc.?
- ✓ Why will customers choose You, Inc. over your competition?
- ✓ Why will your "force multipliers" support and promote You, Inc.?
- ✓ Why will someone decide to become an employee of You, Inc.?
- ✓ Why . . . _____
- ✓ Why . . . _____
- ✓ Why . . . _____

"Who" questions:

- ✓ Who are your initial prospects or customers?
- ✓ Who are your competitors?
- ✓ Who are your initial "force multipliers" and are they in place and ready?
- ✓ Who could be You, Inc.'s second employee?
- ✓ Who . . . _____
- ✓ Who . . . _____
- ✓ Who . . . _____

"How" questions:

- ✓ How much capital—cash on hand—will you need to launch and operate You, Inc.?
- ✓ How do you make You, Inc. legal?
- ✓ How are you going get the word out that You, Inc. is "open for business"?
- ✓ How will you secure your first customer? Your next? And, your next . . . ?
- ✓ How will you motivate, train and lead your employee(s)?
- ✓ How . . . _____
- ✓ How . . . _____
- ✓ How . . . _____

"When" questions:

- ✓ When should specific tasks be completed?
- ✓ When is the right time to contact prospective customers?
- ✓ When should you contact your list of potential "force multipliers"?
- ✓ When should you quit your current job to launch and focus on You, Inc. full-time?

✓ When . . . _____

✓ When . . . _____

✓ When . . . _____

"Where" questions:

✓ Where is the extent of You, Inc.'s local market? Distances from your home or office?

✓ Where will funding for You, Inc. come from—beyond the funds you have in savings?

✓ Where does You, Inc. need to advertise or be visible to draw attention to its service offering?

✓ Where will You, Inc. operate from for its workshop and/or back-office, bookkeeping needs?

✓ Where . . . _____

✓ Where . . . _____

✓ Where . . . _____

As noted earlier, we will be using your answers for the questions above, as well as others, to start You, Inc.'s go-to-market planning. However, before we get into that, I wanted to raise a couple of other topics for you to keep in mind right "from the start."

To be **At Your Best**, You, Inc. needs to have its priorities well-defined and solidly in place.

✓ You, Inc.'s customers and their needs are the center of your universe

✓ You, Inc.'s back-office infrastructure is as vital to success as anything else you do. You cannot neglect it

✓ You, Inc. must be extremely frugal in all its expenses and purchases. Cash is life for You, Inc.

## YOU, INC.'S CUSTOMERS: THE CENTER OF YOUR UNIVERSE

It all starts and ends with You, Inc.'s customers. Sounds a bit dramatic but think about it. Your customers and their level of satisfaction with your services will be the basis on whether You, Inc. lives or dies. The more customers you have and the happier they are, the longer and more profitable the "life" that You, Inc. will enjoy and in turn, that you and yours will enjoy as well.

Now seems like a perfect point to revisit the **At Your Best** concept of "3P+A" and how each element supports your efforts to be **At Your Best** with your customers and prospects.

### *"3P+A" stands for People, Performance, Professionalism & Attitude*

The first "P" is always: **PEOPLE**

◊ *Commit to always give your best efforts toward building solid relationships with your customers, your prospects and your employees—every single time, every single opportunity.*

The next "P" is: **PERFORMANCE**

◊ *Commit to always give your best efforts toward delivering the highest quality work product that you are able to offer—every single time, every single opportunity.*

The final "P" is: **PROFESSIONALISM**

◊ *Commit to always give your best efforts toward being a professional in your work product, behavior and appearance—every single time, every single opportunity.*

The Three Ps are all supported by "A" which stands for: **ATTITUDE**

◊ *Commit to always try to keep a positive, proactive, "can-do" attitude toward whatever comes your way—every single time, every single opportunity.*

Again, remember that there are many things that can and will happen throughout your day that you cannot control. However, there are two things that you can control that will make all the difference in the success of You, Inc.

✓ Only you can control the effort you put into your success
  • Are you putting in your best efforts toward your:
    ◊ People?
    ◊ Performance?
    ◊ Professionalism?
  • Even on those days when you do not feel like it.
✓ Only you can control your attitude
  • Are you letting the "little stuff" of life get in the way of You, Inc.'s success?
  • Attitude is the one thing you can control every day, all day.

---

*If you fail to plan, you are planning to fail!*

—BENJAMIN FRANKLIN

*Plans are worthless, but planning is everything.*

—DWIGHT D. EISENHOWER

---

## YOU, INC.'S GO-TO-MARKET PLAN

As a small business, you need to keep your business planning straightforward and flexible so that as You, Inc. gets off the ground, you can modify your plans according to the reality of the marketplace. Therefore, rather than discussing how to develop an ideal, comprehensive Business Plan, we will be discussing how to develop an action oriented, quick-to-create Go-to-Market Plan. The difference is that the **At Your Best** Go-to-Market Plan is intended to reduce the areas of focus to what I believe are the most critical and non-negotiable requirements for you to do your front-end, go-to-market planning.

The actual form that your plan ends up looking like is completely up to you. However, You, Inc.'s "Go-to-Market Plan" needs to cover three key areas of focus:

| Core Business Strategy | Lay out your vision of You, Inc. as a business and how you plan to go to market |
|---|---|
| | ✓ Define You, Inc.'s position in your local market |
| | • See the next section "Positioning You, Inc." |
| | ✓ Define You, Inc.'s immediate, short-term action plan to enter the market |
| | • See the following section "You, Inc.'s Path to Quick Wins" |

| Timing & Action Plan | Lay out your vision of what needs to be done and by when<br>✓ Define the actions, tasks and milestones that need to be completed, with start and end dates so that you can hold yourself accountable along the way to realizing your plan.<br>　• See the following section "Your Timing & Action Plan" |
|---|---|
| Projected Financials | Lay out your vision for the numbers side of You, Inc.<br>✓ Define the financial projections you expect for—at least—the launch and the first six to twelve months of operation.<br>✓ What are You, Inc.'s startup costs?<br>✓ What is You, Inc.'s Sales Forecast?<br>✓ What is You, Inc.'s Expense Budget?<br>✓ What is You, Inc.'s projected profit or loss?<br>　• Sales (Gross Margin) less Expenses equal Profit or Loss<br>✓ See the following section "For You, Inc., Cash Is Life" |

I want to make one more point about You, Inc.'s Go-to-Market Plan before we get into discussing how to build its component elements. Your plan not only helps you organize and focus your ideas, but it also provides you with an easy-to-share document describing your business. When you need to recruit or enlist the support of or investment from someone, it can help you bolster the credibility of your presentation. You can share with your bankers, vendors, creditors and employees. If you are concerned about protecting sensitive competitive information, like a key client(s) or an important contract, you should consider having recipients of the plan sign a "non-disclosure agreement."

You, Inc.'s Go-to-Market Plan can serve as a document to recruit the best and most talented employees in the market. Everyone wants to be on a team with a vision—from your employees to your banker—everyone wants to be on a winning team.

The planning that you need to do will take time and energy. Often, it may become frustrating to put your ideas on paper. Stay with it. Refine it. But most importantly, finish it. Keep in mind that this has to be a "living" document that you need to revisit, update, modify as your knowledge grows; as your business changes; as opportunities present themselves. A good rule of thumb for yourself should be to review and update You, Inc.'s Go-to-Market Plan at least twice a year. Make time to go through this exercise. It will help you immensely in managing You, Inc. and communicating your business to others.

## ⚒ AYB ASSIST

*Small Time Operator*—"The Business Plan" starting pg. 31
*The Art of the Start*—Chap. 4 "The Art of Writing a Business Plan"

(Remember: the **AYB Assist** gives you a quick reference with specific locations in the recommended books so you can learn more about a topic.)

## YOU, INC.'S MARKET POSITIONING

One of the most important business exercises that you can undertake is to clearly understand how You, Inc., and the services that it offers, fits into your local market. This is commonly referred to as market positioning. The process requires that you be honest with yourself and leave all wishful thinking behind. The more in depth and detailed your understanding of You, Inc.'s true positioning, the better you will be able to develop the plan and strategy to make You, Inc. successful.

This is an excellent opportunity for you to revisit your first SWOT analysis that you built out earlier. Many of the questions and answers that you came up with when you assembled your list of questions under the What, Why, Who, How, When and Where categories will come in handy in defining You, Inc.'s positioning.

Take a few minutes to jot your thoughts below or on a separate sheet of paper. Try to get yourself in the habit of breaking down important business decisions into their component pros and cons—their Strengths, Weaknesses, Opportunities and Threats.

### You, Inc.'s Positioning SWOT Analysis

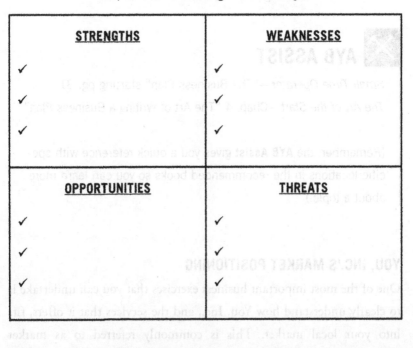

By way of a reminder, here is the same example of a SWOT Analysis for a contractor considering expanding his/her business that we used in Chapter 9 to help you along:

| STRENGTHS | WEAKNESSES |
|---|---|
| ✓ Reputation for quality work<br>✓ Can be super competitive on price due low overhead | ✓ Fine quality takes time<br>✓ Hard to find tradespeople to measure up to my standards |
| **OPPORTUNITIES** | **THREATS** |
| ✓ Only one other fine Craftsman competitor in the market and they are always overbooked<br>✓ My market demographic growth is expected to be 10 percent this year | ✓ Competition may add people to meet the demand<br>✓ You, Inc. competes with other competitors for tradespeople<br>✓ Growth depends on major new plant opening on time. What if? |

**AYB Quick Tool:** Go to www.AtYourBest.com and click on "**AYB Quick Tools**" for a simple, Microsoft Word–based, **SWOT Analysis** worksheet that you can download and easily modify for your purposes. There is also an example of a SWOT Analysis of a business scenario that include a more detailed explanation of the thought process that went into breaking down the situation/decision into its component Strengths, Weaknesses, Opportunities and Threats.

For the purposes of understanding You, Inc.'s market positioning, below are just some of the questions related to how You, Inc. and its service will fit in your local market. You use questions like these to flesh out You, Inc.'s SWOT analysis or feel free to add your own:

✓ What services does You, Inc. plan to offer and why are they competitive?

✓ What differentiates You, Inc. to make its service offering unique or better?

✓ What is the local competitive landscape and how will You, Inc. compete?

✓ What customer needs does You, Inc. address better than its competitors?

✓ Who is the most successful competitor and what are they missing?

✓ Who would be an ideal customer for what You, Inc. will be offering?

✓ What does You, Inc. need to attract its ideal customers?

✓ _____

✓ _____

✓ _____

Once you have exhausted your imagination of the questions related to how You, Inc. and its service offering will fit in your local market and you have considered the Strengths, Weaknesses, Opportunities and Threats associated with those questions, you are ready get down to building out You, Inc.'s Core Business Strategy.

## ✕ AYB ASSIST

*The Art of the Start*—Chap. 2 "The Art of Positioning"

*Guerrilla Marketing Remix*—Chap. 7 "The Guerrilla Marketing Strategy" and Chap. 23 "Guerrilla Research"

(Again, remember **AYB Assist** gives you a quick reference with specific locations in the recommended books so you can learn more about a topic.)

## YOU, INC.'S PATH TO QUICK WINS

You have just gone through the important exercise of defining You, Inc.'s market positioning. You now have a solid understanding of your small business' Strengths, Weaknesses, Opportunities and Threats relative to your local marketplace. We will soon discuss how to lay out a timeline and a list of actions you will need to take to make your plans for You, Inc. a reality. However, right now, I am going to ask you to do a bit of brainstorming on your own.

I believe that it is important to start working toward some immediate results—some quick wins. Quick wins can be small and simple or large and complex. They can be easy or hard to turn into reality. They can be inconsequential or very consequential to the overall scheme of things. The key is that they need to be quick to realize. Some examples of quick wins are:

- ✓ Your new You, Inc. business cards and separate cell phone dedicated to You, Inc. calls
- ✓ A new magnetic sign to put on your pickup truck with You, Inc.'s information printed
- ✓ You, Inc.'s new website with the bare essentials noting that You, Inc. is open for business
- ✓ A small job for your neighbor or friend that you get to invoice under You, Inc.'s name instead of your former employer's
- ✓ A meeting with a prospective supplier, who until your meeting, only knew you as someone else's employee instead of the new CEO of You, Inc.
- ✓ Connecting with an influential force multiplier who want to actively support You, Inc.'s growth

Your objective needs to be to identify as many as you can and prioritize them according to their relative importance to You, Inc. and how quickly you can make them a reality. Then, attack them with a vengeance. Why are quick wins important?

- ✓ Quick wins get you needed attention
- ✓ Quick wins help you gain momentum
- ✓ Quick wins motivate you and your team
- ✓ Quick wins give you the traction you need to go for the next win

I want to ask you to focus exclusively on asking as well as answering yourself additional, immediate-term questions, like the following:

- ✓ What business opportunities exist right now or in the short term, that You, Inc. could turn into quick wins?
- ✓ What opportunities could be uncovered in the short term to convert into quick wins?
- ✓ What actions do you have to take now to make these opportunities a reality?
- ✓ Who are the people that you need to engage in order to make that happen?
- ✓ What resources do you have right now that you can use to make that happen?
- ✓ What resources do you need that you don't have that you can obtain without major investment?

The objective for doing this brainstorming exercise is to help you in the next section—**Your Timing & Action Plan.** The results of this brainstorming session will provide you the raw material you will need to flesh out your plan. Just as importantly it will have you thinking in terms of building early momentum for You, Inc. as you get it off the ground toward realizing you vision of success.

**AYB Quick Tool:** Go to www.AtYourBest.com and click on **"AYB Quick Tools"** for a simple, Microsoft Word–based **Quick Win Brainstorming** worksheet that you can download and easily modify for your purposes.

## YOUR TIMING & ACTION PLAN

Now, you need to put together your **Timing & Action Plan** so you can keep yourself and your team accountable to a definable and measurable process to stay on track. In other words, you need to list out what needs to be accomplished along with a specific time frame for when it needs to be completed and who is responsible.

Ideally, you want to lay out a Timing & Action Plan in chronological order according to three different types of line items. The three types of line items are:

- ✓ **Strategic Objective:** Statements of **What** you want to accomplish
- ✓ **Milestones:** Threshold events or points in time that help you gauge the **When** as You, Inc.'s progresses toward your Strategic Objectives
- ✓ **Tactical Actions or Tasks:** Active steps of **How** you plan to realize your Strategic Objectives and **Who** is responsible

Your Timing & Action Plan can take whatever form works best for you. However, at minimum, your plan should prompt you to list out the objectives, tasks or milestones to be completed; the start by and complete by dates; the cost to complete; and, whether one item is dependent on another item being completed.

Your Timing & Action Plan worksheet will look something like the following:

**Timing & Action Plan for:** _____

| Action, Task or Milestone to Be Completed | Start by Date/ Complete by Date | Who Is Responsible? | Cost to Complete? | Which Other Items Are Dependent on Completion? |
|---|---|---|---|---|
| | | | | |
| | | | | |
| | | | | |

In its simplest form, you should plan to use one Timing & Action Plan worksheet to lay out your top three or four Strategic Objectives for You, Inc. for a specific time frame. Then, for each Strategic Objective, use another Timing & Action Plan worksheet to break down the steps to accomplishing that Strategic Objective into its component Tactical Actions/Tasks and Milestones.

Your objective should be to periodically put everything that you need for a project to do on one or more pages, so you can see what needs to be done and by when. You should review you Timing & Action Plan as often as you need to keep yourself on track toward the You, Inc. launch. Take the time to break down big things into smaller tasks and steps, wherever needed to reduce the size of the target and make things less overwhelming. That way you maximize your opportunity for success without having something slip away from you or drop through the cracks. Try to get yourself in the habit of looking at and tweaking your Timing & Action Plans often so that it becomes a natural extension of your business planning and thinking well into the future.

**AYB Quick Tool:** Go to www.AtYourBest.com and click on "**AYB Quick Tools**" for a simple, Microsoft Excel–based, **Timing & Action Plan** worksheet that you can download and easily modify for your purposes.

---

*Money in the company's bank account is NOT yours! It belongs to your Accounts Payable. Your money starts counting after your A/P, your taxes and your employees are paid.*

—JEFF M., CONTRACTOR

---

## FOR YOU, INC., CASH IS LIFE

For You, Inc., as is the case for any small business, CASH is LIFE. *Without cash, there is no You, Inc.*

- ✓ If You, Inc. does not have enough cash to launch, it dies.
- ✓ If You, Inc. does not have enough cash to market itself, it dies.
- ✓ If You, Inc. does not have enough cash to pay taxes, it dies.
- ✓ If You, Inc. does not have enough cash to pay vendors, it dies.
- ✓ If You, Inc. does not have enough cash to pay creditors, it dies.
- ✓ If You, Inc. does not have enough cash to pay employees, it dies.
- ✓ If You, Inc. has no cash to pay you for long enough, You, Inc. must die.

You get the picture. Cash is life. Without it or when it is in short supply, You, Inc. will be in a world of hurt. In your career, you have no doubt experienced very directly or through a friend, what happens when a small business cannot pay its obligations. Being **At Your Best** as You, Inc., means that you always think about protecting your downside.

Being frugal in all your buying and spending decisions needs to be top of mind and a way of life as you get You, Inc. off the ground. Think twice or three times over before you tap your precious, limited resources on any purchase—for You, Inc. or for yourself. Cash is life for You, Inc.—if it runs out, You, Inc. is dead. This is not an overstatement. It is reality.

Before we continue, I want to strongly encourage you to consider working with a professional accountant/bookkeeper to help you make sure that You, Inc.'s financials are in order—right from the start. If you want to hold off on the accountant/bookkeeper, I fully understand. The following will get you thinking and heading in the right direction.

## ✕ AYB ASSIST

*Small Time Operator*—"Financing" starting pg. 10 and Chap. 2 "Bookkeeping"
*The Art of the Start*—Chap. 5 "The Art of Bootstrapping"
*Guerrilla Marketing Remix*—Chap. 35 "Guerrilla Saving"

## YOU, INC.'S STARTUP FINANCIAL NEEDS

Before you can build a realistic plan as to how You, Inc. can be launched and be successful long term, you need to fully understand the costs of getting You, Inc. off the ground in the first place. The following is a very basic worksheet that you can start with to flesh out the actual financial requirements that You, Inc. will face as a startup.

## You, Inc.'s Startup Financial Requirements:

## EXAMPLE

| STARTUP EXPENSES | |
|---|---|
| Legal Services | $2,000 |
| Printing Services: Cards, Signage & Stationery | $1,000 |
| Cost of Conversion of Your Truck to the You, Inc. Service Truck | $2,500 |
| Ongoing Financing Payments for Truck—first year of You, Inc. | $5,000 |
| Office Equipment | $1,500 |
| Other | $750 |
| **Total Startup Expenses** | **$12,750** |
| STARTUP ASSETS | |
| Cash On Hand—Beyond startup expenses to cover initial cash demands | $20,000 |
| Current Assets—Such as inventory of supplies needed for servicing clients | $5,000 |
| Long Term Assets—Such as your truck and tools | $50,000 |
| Total Startup Assets | $75,000 |
| **Total Financial Requirements To Launch You, Inc.** | **$87,750** |

Whether you use a spreadsheet program or do so on paper, lay out all the possible expenses (one-time and ongoing expenses) that you expect to incur to launch You, Inc. Then itemize the assets you have on hand, such as supplies, tools and your truck or van, as well as the assets you will need going forward.

**AYB Quick Tool:** Go to www.AtYourBest.com and click on **"AYB Quick Tools"** for a simple, Microsoft Excel–based **Startup Expenses** worksheet that you can download and easily modify for your purposes.

## YOU, INC.'S SALES FORECAST

A Sales Forecast at this stage in your go-to-market planning needs to be brutally realistic. Fight off any urges toward wishful thinking. Instead, think in terms of what you truly believe can be accomplished along with the time frames to make it happen. Remember that you have to account for the time it takes to fill your pipeline of prospects and ramp up sales.

In keeping with our theme that "Cash is Life," you need to make it a habit to always look at both the dollar value of a sales transaction, as well as the cost to You, Inc. for that transaction. There are accounting terms and calculations that we could get into here, but I will leave that to you and your accountant/bookkeeper. Right now, however, I want to impress upon you the importance of looking at each sale from a bottom line, profit and loss perspective—your "Gross Margin."

For the purpose of keeping this presentation as clear as possible without turning this into an accounting lesson, I will make one distinction about money spent on behalf of You, Inc. When you spend money to purchase supplies or anything else that will specifically be used to complete a client job, that expenditure is considered a cost of items required to generate sales revenue or a Cost of Goods Sold (COGS). On the other hand, when you spend money on things that help you operate You, Inc., that expenditure is considered an expense.

With that in mind, the following is the beginning of simple Sales Forecast worksheet, so you can envision what creating a Sales Forecast entails.

## You, Inc.'s Sales Forecast:

## EXAMPLE

| PROJECTED SALES REVENUE | Month 1 | Month 2 | Month 3 | Period Total |
|---|---|---|---|---|
| Projected Revenue from Client #1 (Obviously, clients may be different by month) | $1,500 | $2,500 | $2,500 | $6,500 |
| Projected Revenue from Client #2 | $1,000 | $1,500 | $3,500 | $6,000 |
| Projected Revenue from Client #3 | $1,250 | $1,250 | $2,000 | $4,500 |
| Projected Revenue from Client #4 | $0 | $2,500 | $1,000 | $3,500 |
| **Total Projected Monthly Sales Revenue** | **$3,750** | **$7,750** | **$9,000** | **$20,500** |
| **COST OF GOODS SOLD (COGS) PER PROJECTED SALE** | | | | |
| COGS on Sale to Client #1—(COGS equal cost for items required for the sale) | $800 | $1,800 | $1,800 | $4,400 |
| COGS on Sale to Client #2 | $500 | $800 | $2,300 | $3,600 |
| COGS on Sale to Client #3 | $850 | $900 | $1,200 | $2,950 |
| COGS on Sale to Client #4 | $0 | $1,900 | $500 | $2,400 |
| **Subtract Total Projected Monthly Cost of Goods Sold per Sale** | **$2,150** | **$5,400** | **$5,800** | **$13,350** |
| **GROSS MARGIN ON SALES FORECAST** | **$1,600** | **$2,350** | **$3,200** | **$7,150** |

Use your Sales Forecast to build a "pipeline" for your projected sales over the coming months. Try to keep it current and apply as much reality and objectivity to each projected sales. Recognize that it is your responsibility—and yours alone at this stage—to "feed the pipeline." Feeding the pipeline means doing the work to find and secure the next, new client for You, Inc. We will discuss this further in the next chapter "**At Your Best**: Game On."

Make your Sales Forecast a "living," forward-looking document such that once a sale happens or is no longer probable take it off your Sales Forecast. Also, as the months elapse, be sure to keep forward-looking, rolling balances updated to provide the best understanding of You, Inc.'s financial well-being.

**Keep it simple by doing the following:**

✓ Decide on a period of time that you have to track—three or six months or as far out as needed to purchase the supplies required for each client job

✓ Create a period statement for number of months beginning with this month

✓ Swap out the data associated with the most current month that has just elapsed with data associated with the month next in line on your period calendar. In other words, if you have a three-period statement showing Month 1 to Month 3, swap out the data associated with Month 1 and add the data from Month 4 at the end of your statement

✓ Recalculate the totals, review the results and act accordingly until this month elapses. Then, do it again

Create a rolling period statement swapping out an "old" month's data with a new month's information, so you can keep yourself and You, Inc.'s financials in line with the ongoing reality of the marketplace.

**AYB Quick Tool:** Go to www.AtYourBest.com and click on "**AYB Quick Tools**" for a simple, Microsoft Excel–based **Sales Forecast** worksheet that you can download and easily modify for your purposes. Also, included are examples on how to turn your Sales Forecast into a "living" document and reality-based "pipeline" of future business.

---

*Credit today is negative cashflow next month.*

—GARTH B., CONTRACTOR, ATLANTA

---

## YOU, INC.'S EXPENSE BUDGET

As with your Sales Forecast, your projected Expense Budget needs to be as brutally realistic and detailed as you can make it to fully understand and protect your downside. Again, remember differentiate "Expenses" from "Cost of Goods Sold" by asking yourself, "Is this expenditure required for a specific client job or for operating You, Inc.?" If your answer is the latter, it is an expense. Here is a very simple Expense Budget worksheet that you can use to think through what your projected expenses will be.

## You, Inc.'s Expense Budget:

## EXAMPLE

| PROJECTED EXPENSES | Month 1 | Month 2 | Month 3 | Period Total |
|---|---|---|---|---|
| Rent—for now will assume You, Inc. operates from a home office | $0 | $0 | $0 | $0 |
| Payroll—your income and related taxes plus any other employees | $0 | $250 | $1,000 | $1,250 |
| Office/workshop related—itemize in detail where possible | $350 | $350 | $350 | $1,050 |
| Insurance | $500 | $500 | $500 | $1,500 |
| Vehicle Related—itemize in detail where possible | $750 | $750 | $750 | $2,250 |
| Other—itemize in detail where possible | $350 | $500 | $500 | $1,350 |
| TOTAL PROJECTED EXPENSES | $1,950 | $2,350 | $3,100 | $7,400 |

Use your Expense Budget to build a picture of your projected expenditures over the coming months. Try to keep it current and apply as much reality and objectivity to each projected expenditure—even to the point of rounding up on any estimate to further protect your downside. As we did earlier with the Sales Forecast, make the Expense Budget a "living" document such that once an expense takes place or is no longer probable you make the appropriate change. Finally, as the months elapse, be sure to move your running tally looking forward so you can keep yourself and You, Inc.'s financials in line with the reality of the marketplace.

**AYB Quick Tool:** Go to www.AtYourBest.com and click on "**AYB Quick Tools**" for a simple, Microsoft Excel–based **Expense Budget** worksheet that you can download and easily modify for your purposes. Also, included are examples on how to turn your Expense Budget into a "living" document.

## YOU, INC.'S PROFIT & LOSS STATEMENT

Now, you are ready to combine the results of your Sales Forecast with those from your projected Expense Budget to create your projected Profit & Loss Statement. As with the Sales Forecast and the Expense Budget, You, Inc.'s needs to be a "living" document as well.

### You, Inc.'s Profit & Loss Statement:
### EXAMPLE

| PROFIT & LOSS STATEMENT | Month 1 | Month 2 | Month 3 | Period Total |
|---|---|---|---|---|
| **Sales Forecast** | | | | |
| Projected Sales Revenue | $3,750 | $7,750 | $9,000 | $20,500 |
| Less Cost of Goods Sold | $2,150 | $5,400 | $5,800 | $13,350 |
| **Total Projected Gross Margin on Sales** | **$1,600** | **$2,350** | **$3,200** | **$7,150** |
| **Expense Budget** | | | | |
| Less Projected Expenses | $1950 | $2350 | $3,100 | $7400 |
| **PROJECTED PROFIT OR LOSS** | **- $350** | **$0** | **$100** | **- $250** |

In the scenario above, You, Inc. is projected to lose money in Month 1; to break even in Month 2; and, make a bit of money in Month 3. However, overall during the period, You, Inc. is expected to lose money due to the slow start in Month 1. You want to make sure that you are keeping a very close watch on your current and projected Profit & Loss Statement to avoid being surprised. Doing so, is the only way, you can protect your downside and ensure You, Inc.'s success. Not doing so, is the surest path to ensuring You, Inc.'s demise.

**AYB Quick Tool:** Go to www.AtYourBest.com and click on "**AYB Quick Tools**" for a simple, Microsoft Excel–based **Profit & Loss Statement** worksheet that you can download and easily modify for your purposes. Also, included are examples on how to turn your Expense Budget into a "living" document.

## FINANCING YOU, INC.

Now that you have a clear understanding of what you need to launch and operate You, Inc., you need to decide how you will finance the launch. Here are your probable financing choices:

| | |
|---|---|
| **Self-Financing** | You put up your own money to finance the launch of You, Inc. with your savings and your net worth. Self-financing gives you the greatest amount of control over what to do and how to do with the financing used for You, Inc. |
| **Debt Financing** | You borrow some or all of the funds needed to launch You, Inc. Debt financing means that you will someday need to pay back the principal loan as well as make interest payments along the way. Loans, typically, come with wide ranges of possible requirements or restrictions, depending on whether the loan is a personal loan from friends or |

family, or from a bank or other type of lender. Interest paid on financing comes directly out of your profit.

**Equity Financing**    You join forces with someone else, who, in return for an ownership stake in You, Inc., provides you funds needed to launch You, Inc. Equity financing means an investor. An investor means a co-owner. A co-owner means giving up a share of profits and a measure of control.

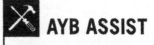

## AYB ASSIST

*Small Time Operator*—"Financing" starting pg. 10

*The Art of the Start*—Chap. 4 "The Art of Writing a Business Plan"

## YOU, INC.'S BACK-OFFICE INFRASTRUCTURE

Before you can legitimately launch You, Inc., you need to have your "house in order" or else you will probably encounter an ugly array of organizational, legal and financial problems. In other words, at the very minimum, you should to take action on the following before you accept your first paying customer:

✓ You, Inc.'s and your professional local and state business licenses and permits must be up-to-date

✓ You, Inc.'s Federal Employer Identification Number and your Social Security number will be needed

✓ You, Inc.'s and your personal insurance coverage need to be in line with your future plans

✓ You, Inc.'s business accounts and your personal bank and credit accounts need to be kept separate and apart

✓ You need to have a bookkeeping system in place that allows you to easily capture and keep track of every transaction and document associated with each You, Inc. customer, vendor, employee, asset or liability

We will discuss these further in the coming sections. However, as we get ready to discuss your go-to-market planning, you should already be thinking about how you will set a solid foundation with your back-office infrastructure.

## 🪓 AYB ASSIST

*Small Time Operator*—
"Licenses and Permits" pg. 10,
"Federal Identification Numbers" pg. 23,
"Insurance" pg. 26 and
Chap. 2 "Bookkeeping"—(*Please* read Chapter 2.)

## "LICENSED, BONDED & INSURED"

Each state in the US has a widely different and evolving set of requirements for businesses to operate in the Skilled Trades. These requirements are designed to inform and protect consumers from fraud, damages and liability. Often, one of the first discussion items that you will need to address with a prospective client will be to confirm that You, Inc. is "Licensed, Bonded & Insured." The following provides a brief explanation of these terms.

## Licensed

Most states and some local governments offer contractor's licenses. Licenses are granted upon showing that you compile with the requirements specified. You are then expected to display your license number on your business card, marketing materials, website, etcetera. If a license is available in your area, you should definitely pursue it. Not only does the license add to You, Inc.'s sense of professionalism, but it also can help you collect damages if a client refuses to pay. Also, many states have public websites that provide consumers a quick but important reference to verify a contractor's information and credibility as a business.

## Bonded

A bonded contractor has established a surety bond, which is typically required with getting a license or signing up to be granted a building permit. When you apply for a state license you will also be required to purchase a "license and permit bond." These bonds guarantee that you will pay financial damages if your work does not meet license and permit standards.

## Insured

By advertising that You, Inc. is insured, it means that you have general liability insurance in place in the event a client files a lawsuit resulting from services provided or promised by You, Inc. General liability insurance covers legal expenses and damages resulting from such a lawsuit.

**AYB Quick Tool:** Go to www.AtYourBest.com and click on "**AYB Quick Tools**" for an up-to-date, Microsoft Word–based "Licensing Information Websites"—a by-State list of agency or department websites that provide the specific licensing requirements for each US State and Territory.

## WHICH LEGAL STRUCTURE IS RIGHT FOR YOU, INC.?

The correct legal business structure depends on your business objectives and your concerns about protecting your personal assets. As a small business in the Skilled Trades, you have a number of choices.

### Sole Proprietorship

A Sole Proprietorship is the simplest and least costly (at least in the beginning) business structure to set up.

- ✓ Your business income is reported on your personal income tax form
- ✓   Your personal assets are not protected
  - • If your business runs into trouble, everything that you own of value could be at risk

### Partnership

A Partnership is like a marriage: There is good but there is also bad, especially if there is a breakup.

- ✓ It is like a Sole Proprietorship with more owners
- ✓ Income is divided according to a predecided ratio among the partners and is reported on their personal income tax forms
- ✓ The partners' personal assets are not protected
  - • If the business runs into trouble, everything of value that is owned by the partners—personally—may be at risk
- ✓ In the event that the business is dissolved, the debts and assets are divided among the partners—hopefully, according to a prearranged formula

## *Limited Liability Corporation (LLC)*

A Limited Liability Corporation allows even a one-person business to incorporate to protect their personal assets.

- ✓ Your business income is still reported on your personal income taxes but now it is referred to as "pass-through business income" which may be taxed at a more attractive rate
- ✓ You have to register your LLC with your state
- ✓ Your personal assets are protected from those of your company
  - If your business runs into trouble, your personal assets will not be at risk, as long as the trouble in question does not involve:
    - ◊ Failure to deposit taxes withheld from employees
    - ◊ Commingling business and personal finances
    - ◊ Fraud

## *S-Corporation*

An S-Corporation is more complex and costly to set up than an LLC but it offers additional tax benefits to you and your company.

- ✓ Your business income is reported on your personal income taxes as "pass-through business income" which will be taxed at a more attractive rate
- ✓ As the owner of the business, you are paid a salary and can earn bonuses against which the company withholds employee related taxes thereby reducing your tax burden allowing the company to write off a portion of those employee taxes
- ✓ As under the LLC structure, your personal assets will be legally protected

**My recommendation:** A Sole Proprietorship or a Partnership may be the easiest, fastest and least costly structures to set up initially, but they carry some inherent risks that are discussed above. My strong recommendation to you is that you seriously consider setting up a Limited Liability Corporation (LLC) for You, Inc. to give several important legal protections.

### Formalizing You, Inc.'s Legal Structure

When you have decided on appropriate legal structure for You, Inc., you will want to have it formalized. At this early stage, the process and costs associated with formalizing the legal structure of You, Inc. will not be significant—certainly not when compared to costs and issues associated with not doing so at all. You can speak with a local attorney to draw up the necessary documents or you can use an online legal service such as LegalZoom and Rocket Lawyer.

Either LegalZoom or Rocket Lawyer provides you a quick, inexpensive, online approach to setting up You, Inc. Go to www.LegalZoom.com and click on "Business Formation" and/or go to www.RocketLawyer.com and click on "Business." It will take you through a straightforward step-by-step process.

### ✖ AYB ASSIST

*Small Time Operator*—"Legal Structure" pg. 15 and "You, Incorporated" pg. 83

# CHAPTER 10 REPLAY
## At Your Best: The Kick Off

» To be **At Your Best** from the start, you will need to ask and answer many questions, which can put into six categories: What, Why, Who, How, When and Where. An example of each would be:
  - What is a realistic Sales Forecast for You, Inc.?
  - Why is now the right time to launch You, Inc.?
  - Who are your initial prospects or customers?
  - How much capital—cash on hand—will you need to launch and operate You, Inc.?
  - When should specific tasks be completed?
  - Where is the extent of You, Inc.'s local market?

» You, Inc.'s customers need to be the center of your universe.
  - Use 3P+A to be **At Your Best** with your customers and prospects

» You, Inc.'s Go-To-Market Plan needs to be comprised of three key components:
  - Core Business Strategy
  - Timing & Action Plan
  - Projected Financials

» Defining You, Inc.'s market positioning is an important business planning exercise to help you understand clearly how You, Inc. and the services you offer fit into your local market

» Quick wins help you see immediate results and start your momentum
  - Identify the areas and tasks that you can turn into a quick win and make it happen

» Build your Timing & Action Plan
  - Strategic objective—what you want to accomplish

- Milestones—when you will complete threshold events
- Tactical actions and tasks—how you will accomplish the elements of the objective and who is responsible

» For You, Inc., cash is life. You need to think through the financial aspects of launching You, Inc.

- Start-up financial requirements
- Sales forecasting
- Expense budgeting
- Profit & Loss Statement

» You need to set up You, Inc. as a legal entity and put together its back-office infrastructure

# At Your Best: Game On

# YOU ARE AT YOUR BEST
## *delivering the highest-level customer service and quality work product.*

---

## AT YOUR BEST ON THE FIELD

Congratulations! You have launched your business and You, Inc. has its first paying customers. That is a tremendous milestone that so many others never reach. Now, you want to continue to differentiate yourself and You, Inc. You want to avoid the ugly fate that large percentages of small businesses meet because they did not focus on the critical success factors that would have kept them going and growing. By way of a recap, those critical success factors typically are:

✓ Consistent Delivery of High Quality Service
✓ Focus on Customer Service and Loyalty
✓ Financial and Cash Flow Management
✓ Effectiveness of Business Operation and Processes
✓ Success in Sales and Marketing
✓ Small Team Leadership

You need to stay on top of these critical success factors. You have to spend whatever time needed to drill down on any issue that is not quite right. You need to be able to answer and/or take action on the following questions:

- ✓ What actions are you taking to always put your customers first?
- ✓ Are you turning each customer into a "Raving Fan" for You, Inc.? (More on "Raving Fans" shortly.)
- ✓ What is your cash position and what are the expenses against it, today; or this week; or next week or month?
- ✓ Are you being frugal with your expenditures, keeping your Expense Budget less than your Sales Forecast?
- ✓ Are you presenting a professional and high-quality impression in every customer interaction? If not, why and how will you fix that?
- ✓ What are you doing to get your next customer? And, the next? Are you "feeding the pipeline"?
- ✓ Have you gotten your initial set of "force multipliers" in place and are they championing You, Inc.?
- ✓ Is your back-office, record-keeping process helping you stay on track? Do you need someone to help you?
- ✓ How are you tracking against your original Go-to-Market Plans? What changes should you make?
- ✓ Remember, whatever "it" is . . . Ask, is it realistic? Did you SWOT it?

## CUSTOMER SERVICE: YOUR COMPETITIVE ADVANTAGE

As you launch and work to get You, Inc. underway, you are going to have to compete with other firms in your local market. They may be more established, or they may undercut your pricing, or they may simply be there first. You, Inc. has the opportunity to differentiate itself right from the start by focusing on delivering the highest possible customer service.

Nothing will differentiate You, Inc. more clearly from all your competition than if You, Inc. consistently delivers excellent customer service. Excellent customer service is not something clients expect anymore because they have grown accustomed to not getting it from service providers in any industry. Unfortunately, people have come to expect bad or mediocre customer service. My definition of "excellent customer service" is: consistently providing your customers a level of service that exceeds their expectations—going "above and beyond" so much so that they become your advocate.

Unfortunately, nowadays excellent customer service is an exception not a rule. When any client actually experiences excellent customer service it is a memorable surprise—one that they usually recount to their friends and family. Imagine the impact on your clients' perception of You, Inc.'s customer service and on You, Inc's business, if you actively looked for ways to surprise and delight your customers in every interaction.

Think about it in your own life. Think about how seldomly you see excellent customer service happen and how good it makes you feel when you do experience it and want to return. Make excellent customer service You, Inc.'s unassailable competitive advantage. Turn You, Inc.'s customers into "Raving Fans."

*Raving Fans* is the title of a short, unique book written by Ken Blanchard and Sheldon Bowles. It is a very, quick read (132 pages) that will fundamentally change your perspective on how to establish and build solid, long-lasting relationships with your customers, turning them into "Raving Fans" for You, Inc.

I cannot recommend **any more strongly** that you take the opportunity to read *Raving Fans*. Again, it is a very short, unique and quirky book and it's a very fast read. It is written as a humorous parable to apply to any size business in any industry. Your "guide" and one of book's main characters is a Fairy Godmother, who happens to be a golf-loving male. Still, you will learn some critically important lessons that, in turn, could become You, Inc.'s most effective, unbeatable, competitive advantages as you build your small business.

In the briefest terms, *Raving Fans* walks you through its three "secret rules" for turning customers into "Raving Fans."

## Rule #1: "Decide on What You Want."

Establish your own vision of what you believe that excellent customer service should look like for You, Inc. Decide on what you believe constitutes the elements of the You, Inc. customer service experience that you want to present to your local market that will differentiate You, Inc. from the competitors.

## Rule #2: "Discover What the Customer Wants."

Actively engage your customers to learn what their views and expectations of excellent customer service might look like by asking them directly about their experience with You, Inc. Recognize that if they remain silent or simply say, "It's fine," you better ask more questions because they probably are not the least bit satisfied. Be ready and open to their suggestions or criticisms and do not get defensive. Your objective is to compare what the customer wants with your vision and determine what changes you might need to make to your vision.

## Rule #3: "Deliver the Vision Plus 1 Percent."

Consistently deliver on your vision of excellent customer service taking into account your customers' expectations. Focus on those elements of your vision that you know You, Inc. can deliver no matter what and set expectations accordingly. Then, push You, Inc. to go beyond by committing to continually improving a bit at a time—just 1 percent better—in order to get closer and closer to your full vision of excellent customer service.

## AT YOUR BEST WITH FORCE MULTIPLIERS

In Part 2 of this AYB Playbook, we discussed how force multipliers magnify You, Inc.'s reach in your efforts to find a job. Now, with You, Inc. as a small business, you need to think in terms of how to make You, Inc. look and act bigger than reality. You want to always try to make an outsized—positive—impact on your clients, on your contractors and in your market to drive the growth and success of You, Inc. The most effective way to do so is to build relationships with key "force multipliers."

**A Reminder:** A potential force multiplier is any person or business whose market position gives them access to customers and prospects that you would love to have as You, Inc.'s customers and prospects. A force multiplier could be:

- ✓ The best general contractor(s) that you ever worked for
- ✓ The mentor, who "took you under his wing" when you were first starting out
- ✓ The hardware, supplies and equipment vendors within 10–15 miles of your local market
- ✓ The top five realtors in your community, who are always asked for their opinion on service providers
- ✓ The top five architecture and engineering firms in town, who are always looking for excellent contractors
- ✓ The owner of the most commonly seen fleet of service trucks that you see when you are driving in town

✓ The deacon at your church, who also happens to be the head of a local builders' association

✓ Anyone with whom a relationship would give You, Inc. access to clients that would otherwise be out of reach

## GROWING YOU, INC.'S BUSINESS THROUGH NETWORKING

You have built your career with the mindset of a Craftsman and a commitment to be **At Your Best**. You now need to get the word out that You, Inc. is striking out on its own. You need to "network" to establish and build relationships with the force multipliers, who will extend You, Inc.'s reach and opportunities for success. The thing is that "networking" does not mean meeting people and hoping that they will like you enough to magically recommend You, Inc.

True, effective networking only results from being the type of person or business that others want to meet and/or recommend. It comes down to the fact that people will only really want to meet or recommend You, Inc., if You, Inc. has something unique and of value to offer AND if You, Inc. will make them look good in the process.

**Bottom line:** Effective networking needed to build your "team" of force multipliers comes down to focusing on trying to answer the following question: What is in it for them? It does not and cannot come from focusing on trying to answer: What is in it for yourself? "What's in it for you?" will come in due course as long as you give each person or business in your network the reasons to want to be your trusted force multiplier.

This is not a one-and-done thing. The more "seeds" you plant— securing force multipliers ready to advocate on You, Inc.'s behalf—the broader and deeper will be your potential market penetration. Remember: It is all about what's in it for them. Look for opportunities to ask: "How can I be helpful to you?" You have to make a consistent, honest invest-ment in making it worthwhile for them to want to associate themselves and their business credibility with You, Inc.

The good thing is that you are already well on your way there. You have a plan and you are **At Your Best**. Now, it is time to put You, Inc. top-of-mind with your key force multipliers. Build your network of force multipliers by being **At Your Best**.

## ⚒ AYB ASSIST

*Guerrilla Marketing Remix*—Chap. 38 "Guerrilla Networking"
*The Art of the Start*—Chap. 8 "The Art of Partnering"

## YOU, INC.'S VP OF SALES & BUSINESS DEVELOPMENT

You, Inc. will thrive and grow in direct correlation to your ability and commitment to identify new customers and generate sales. It may not be your strong suit but you need to embrace your inner salesperson. The difference between mediocrity and excellence depends on you. You need to see yourself as the driver of new business for You, Inc.

There is no doubt that there is a shortage across the US for trained people and firms in the Skilled Trades. By its very nature, a shortage represents an opportunity for anyone, who is qualified, to meet the demand. The question is whether you plan to meet that demand by pas-sively waiting for your phone to ring or by actively seeking out your opportunities to succeed.

I strongly recommend that you take on and embrace the role of "VP of Sales & Business Development" with enthusiasm and passion. It is your job to "feed the pipeline." Feeding You, Inc.'s pipeline means building a steady stream of prospective customers from which you will potentially get revenue.

As the VP of Sales & Business Development, you must focus on:

- ✓ Understanding the customers' needs and offering them solutions and support
- ✓ Identifying, qualifying and closing customer sales opportunities
- ✓ Building relationships with current and potential customers for possible future business
- ✓ Creating and executing targeted, proactive sales and prospecting strategies to build a pipeline for future business
- ✓ Establishing and building win-win relationships with other complementary businesses and "force multipliers"

Think about what this role entails and how it is all about driving business—all while you are keeping on top of current business, customers and employees. Again, embrace the role and make it your mission going forward.

## ⚒ AYB ASSIST

*Guerrilla Marketing Remix*—Chap. 44 "Guerrilla Selling"
*The Art of the Start*—Chap. 10 "The Art of Rainmaking"

## GETTING THE WORD OUT

For You, Inc. to have customers, you first, have to get the word out that You, Inc. is "Open For Business!" In the preceding section—The Kick Off—we discussed You, Inc.'s market positioning. You were encouraged to do a SWOT analysis to lay out You, Inc.'s Strengths, Weaknesses,

Opportunities and Threats. Now, let's put your work on You, Inc.'s positioning to use.

Again, as a small business owner, you are both the CEO and the VP of Sales & Business Development. It is your job to get the word out. You will want to think through how to present You, Inc. and its service offering in a manner that gives the listener a clear understanding of what You, Inc. offers and why it is different and better than the competition. One tried-and-true way to do that is to create your "elevator pitch" for You, Inc.'s business.

Although we have discussed creating an elevator pitch earlier in this AYB Playbook, we are going to get into a bit more detail here. An elevator pitch is a brief (20–30 seconds), persuasive set of talking points that you can use to spark the interest of your listener(s). You will want to practice your elevator pitch often—even in front of a mirror—to have it seem perfectly natural as you talk about You, Inc. and why your listener should consider using or recommending You, Inc.

The parts of an effective elevator pitch are easy to describe. However, they are less easy to actually build out because you need to think through what you want to say without spending too much time on any one area. Your overall objective is to say just enough to capture the listeners' attention so that they give you feedback and ask you for more information. Just as importantly, you need to know your audience and tailor your elevator pitch to make appropriate for them versus trying to come up with a one-size-fits-all approach.

Here are the steps to create your elevator pitch:

1. **Define your goal clearly.** You want to tell prospective customers, "force multipliers," or anyone else about You, Inc.; you want to introduce a new service offering; or you want to let folks know about something else.

2. **Explain what You, Inc. does.** You want to clearly state that You, Inc. is a new player in your local market and you are there to meet the need not being met by your competition.

3. **Describe You, Inc.'s unique selling proposition.** You want to let the listener know that through either your attention to your craft; or, through your commitment to excellent customer service; or, through your on-time, on-budget delivery of service; or, through some other way You, Inc. is unique in the market.

4. **Engage your listener with a closing question.** You want to ask a question to have the listener provide you feedback on your elevator pitch. Make sure that your closing question is open-ended instead of a question that can be answered with a "yes" or "no." For instance, you could ask, "How do you think that You, Inc. could possibly help you in the near future?" Or, maybe ask, "Who do you recommend that I contact that could use You, Inc. services?"

5. **Put #2, #3 and #4 together.** You should now have a set of talking points—three or four sentences and a closing question—that lays out what You, Inc. does, what makes it unique, and a question engaging the listener to volunteer their feedback on how You, Inc. might be of service to them or someone they know.

6. **Practice, practice, practice.** You want to make giving your elevator pitch as natural as telling somebody your name and address. The more you practice the easier it will be for you to have your elevator pitch at the ready for any opportunity to get the word out.

Now, get out there and get the word out that You, Inc. is open for business.

✓ Actively seek out opportunities to give your elevator pitch to someone new

✓ Set a goal for yourself to meet two or three new people every day to whom you can give your elevator pitch and ask, "How do you think that You, Inc. could help you or someone you know in the near future?"

✓ Always, always keep a few fresh and professionally printed You, Inc. business cards available to hand out to a prospective client or force multiplier

One approach that you might consider is to use the Timing & Action Plan worksheet to create a plan for your business development, outreach strategy to get the word out that You, Inc. is open for business.

✓ List out your objectives, the individual tasks that need to be accomplished and the milestone to need to be met along with the dates by which they need to be completed

✓ Be as detailed as you can to break these down to give yourself and your team daily or weekly targets to hit for meetings or visits or new people to meet or whatever it takes

✓ Keep the plan with you or readily available so that you can keep it top of mind in your daily life

✓ Hold yourself and your team accountable to completing the items listed so you can cross them off and move on to the next one

✓ Be consistent, professional and be persistent

**Bottom line:** It is up to you to make You, Inc. successful. Decide and make it happen by holding yourself accountable to your harshest critic—yourself.

**AYB Quick Tool:** Go to www.AtYourBest.com and click on "**AYB Quick Tools.**" for a Microsoft Word–based, **Elevator Pitch** worksheet to develop your own elevator pitch. Also, you will find the Microsoft Excel-based **Timing & Action Plan** worksheet there, along with an example of how to use it for your business development outreach activities.

## AYB ASSIST

*Guerrilla Marketing Remix*—Chap. 44 "Guerrilla Selling"
*The Art of the Start*—Chap. 10 "The Art of Rainmaking"

## CUSTOMER LEADS & REVIEWS ON THE WEB

One of the most effective ways to "Get the Word Out" is to have your customers do it for you on the Internet. Your customers can be a tremendous source of new customer leads by simply going onto the Web and giving their opinion of You, Inc. and its services. The most prominent online review and rating services for contractors are **Angie's List** and **Home Advisor**, although other sites exist. The reviews on these types of sites can be a double-edged sword given that you cannot control what is said and how you are rated. However, if you operate on a basis of always being **At Your Best**, that sword should always be cutting in your favor.

Many, many of your prospective customers are going to visit one of these sites *before* they call you out of the blue or you get a call back from your outreach. These online services act as both a customer referral system and a means by which prospective clients can do their due diligence on You, Inc. Ignore them at your own peril. There is real business to be had from cultivating your presence on these online review sites, which always starts with delivering the best quality work product and giving excellent customer service.

Given that these online services continually update their websites and processes, we will not lay out how to specifically guide your clients to post their reviews and ratings on behalf of You, Inc. Suffice it to say that you want to encourage them to do so. You, Inc.'s unbeatable, competitive advantage is its consistent, excellent customer service. Take advantage of that. Get your clients to boast about the great customer service offered by You, Inc. and have it work in your favor—at no cost to you.

**AYB Quick Tools:** Go to www.AtYourBest.com and click on "**AYB Quick Tools**" for a Client **How-to-do Ratings** sheet—with easy-to-follow, up-to-date instructions that you can hand out to your happy customers so they can go onto the Angie's List and Home Advisor websites to give their review and rating of You, Inc.'s excellent customer service.

## TABLE STAKES MARKETING TOOLKIT

As a small business, resources are always going to be tight, especially until You, Inc. is running with a steady stream of new and returning customers and the resulting revenue. Therefore, it is critical that you give You, Inc. its best chance of success with a well-executed marketing action plan or strategy to create that consistent stream of customers and revenue. The thing is that "marketing" means many things depending on who you ask and whatever definition you get, comes with a price tag.

For the purposes of being **At Your Best** as a new, self-employed small business in the Skilled Trades, I believe that you need to think in terms of "table stakes marketing." In business, "table stakes" means the minimum set of requirements to pursue or enter a business arrangement. For You, Inc., those table stakes include your skills and reputation as a Craftsman, your tools of the trade needed to do the job at hand and your marketing "tools" that present You, Inc.'s image to your customers, prospects and force multipliers as professional and credible. This last element of the table stakes for You, Inc., represents the minimum set of marketing tools that you should plan to have in place as you build your new small business.

Whether you assemble your own marketing tools, or you use those available via the **AYB Quick Tool**, You, Inc.'s Table Stakes Marketing Toolkit include:

## You, Inc. Business Card
You need presentable and professionally printed business cards available at all times that includes:
- ✓ Your business' name
- ✓ Your name
- ✓ Your business phone number
- ✓ Your business email address
- ✓ Your mailing address

## You, Inc. Phone Number
You need a business phone number that is separate and different than your personal phone
- ✓ Your business phone should have voice messaging and call forwarding capabilities—at minimum

## You, Inc. Email Address
You need a business email address that is separate and different from your personal email
- ✓ You should plan to use the simple email folder organization process to help you manage your business email correspondence with folders for each client, prospect, supplier, creditor and

employee, just to name a few possible categories of folders to organize emails separately.

## You, Inc. Mailing Address

You need a business mailing address that is separate and different from your home address

- ✓ You can sign up for an inexpensive mail box that will allow you keep your business and personal affairs separate, while presenting a more professional image

## You, Inc. Forms & Stationery

You need professional looking forms and stationery for use with clients, prospects and others

- ✓ You can have all the forms, like invoices, estimates for services, advertising flyers and blank letters, as templates in electronic form so you can modify each form as required.

## You, Inc. Website

You need to establish a business website presence for You, Inc.

- ✓ You can have a basic website up and running very inexpensively and quickly. Your website can simply provide the necessary overview information about You, Inc. to convey the credibility you need when dealing with your prospects, customers, vendors and the general public.

## You, Inc. Elevator Pitch(es)

You need to be able to easily and quickly communicate You, Inc.'s **business value proposition** and what you offer

- ✓ You should have a clear and easy-to-understand set of talking points that you can rely on to speak to anyone about You, Inc.

**AYB Quick Tool:** Go to www.AtYourBest.com and click on "**AYB Quick Tools**" for easy-to-follow, up-to-date instructions on how to build out your **Table Stakes Marketing Toolkit**

The AYB Table Stakes Marketing Toolkit consists of the following tools, worksheets, and templates:

- ✓ **You, Inc. Business Card:** A Microsoft Word–based template that you can use to easily insert your specific information and hand off to a professional printer or an online business card production service
- ✓ **You, Inc. Business Mailing Address:** A breakdown of how to set up a separate, business-only mailing address with a link to set up a post office box with your local US Post Office or a link to find your local UPS Store where you set up a mailing address with a street address, which might suit your purposes better
- ✓ **You, Inc. Business Email Address:** A step-by-step approach to creating a new email address for You, Inc. using Google's Gmail. Obviously, there are many alternatives to Gmail and you are encouraged to do what you believe is best for You, Inc.
- ✓ **You, Inc. Forms & Stationery:** A set of easy-to-use Microsoft Word–based templates designed to be modified quickly to give You, Inc.'s correspondence and business forms a professional look in all its correspondence with clients, prospects and the marketplace.
- ✓ **You, Inc. Business Website:** An up-to-date, process description for setting up a basic website for You, Inc. **Please note:** There are many website creation approaches that you can take to accomplish the same objective. The instructions presented will be for the most easy-to-use, online service that I can find to create You, Inc.'s essential web presence in the least costly and most

straightforward manner. These instructions can be expected to change over time, so you should download the most current version of the Toolkit before you begin

✓ **Elevator Pitch:** A Microsoft Word–based worksheet to develop your own elevator pitch

## YOU, INC., TECHNOLOGY & RUNNING YOUR BUSINESS

Technology is everywhere. So much of it can be distracting and a waste of time. However, there are technology solutions that could make a world of difference in helping you grow You, Inc. I will only touch on a few areas that I believe could immediately help you impact You, Inc.'s effectiveness.

### Your Smartphone

Your smartphone can become an incredibly powerful business tool used to support your efforts to build You, Inc.

✓ You can use it to quickly take and send a picture to a client of a problem that you just uncovered so they are aware of it and you don't have to delay the work

✓ You or members of your team can use to take an image or video of an issue that you may be working on and share it with a more experienced Craftsman, who may not be near your jobsite but who has the knowledge you need to address the matter at hand

✓ You can use it to manage all You, Inc.'s critical business processes while on the go

Your smartphone and the wide array of business apps available can magnify your effectiveness at little cost. Below are just a small sample of the mobile tools readily available on your device.

### Finance and Accounting

You can manage all You, Inc.'s financial tasks, including invoicing, payroll and taxes so that you have a clear and full picture of You, Inc.'s financial health. These solutions are easy to use and are very inexpensive, especially given the tremendous value to You, Inc. Take a look at:

- ✓ QuickBooks at www.QuickBooks.com
- ✓ FreshBooks at www.FreshBooks.com

### Time Tracking and Billing

Depending on how you plan to evolve your business, time management, and billing your clients may become a requirement. There are some excellent time tracking solutions, some of which can be integrated with your accounting system. Consider:

- ✓ TSheets at www.TSheets.com which integrates directly with QuickBooks
- ✓ Dovico at www.Dovico.com also integrates with QuickBooks as well as with Microsoft Excel

### Job Estimating

If you are ready to expand beyond tracking time spent on a project and move onto estimating and managing bids on proposed jobs, there is a mobile app for that as well. These too are designed to be easy-to-use and inexpensive. Look at:

- ✓ JobFLEX at www.Job-FLEX.com

## Managing Payments

Mobile payment apps enable You, Inc. to accept payment upon completion or delivery of your work product. These solutions offer an easy-to-use credit card reader that can be connected to a smartphone or mobile device to execute the payment. The value to you and to your customer for the convenience and immediate resolution of a transaction cannot be understated. Take a look at:

✓ PayPal Here at www.PayPal.com
✓ Square at www.SquareUp.com

## Personal Organization

You may have a need to create and manage to-do lists, projects, reminders, and notes, as well as share them with your clients and/or future employees. Using your mobile devices to keep yourself organized is becoming easier and easier, as is sharing your results. A number of task organizing apps, exist but consider:

✓ Evernote at www.Evernote.com
✓ Trello at www.Trello.com

## General Reference

You can always use a quick reference when you are on a job site. Here is a FREE app that might come in handy when you need it most. It is a full-scale construction and reference tool that comes stocked with the construction calculators and materials you need to get the job done.

✓ DEWALT Mobile Pro at Google Play or on iTunes or at www
.Dewalt.cengage.com/mobilepro/free-construction-calculator

## _____ CHAPTER 11 REPLAY _____
### At Your Best: Game On

» You, Inc. can establish a critically important competitive advantage with every customer interaction by consistently delivering the highest-level customer service and quality work product to build customer loyalty and extend You, Inc.'s market reach through word-of-mouth referrals

» Grow You, Inc.'s business through effective networking with your "team" of force multipliers to leverage their access to their customers, friends and acquaintances

» You need to actively embrace your role as VP of Sales and Business Development to get the word out that You, Inc. is "open for business"
  • Always be looking to identify new business opportunities for You, Inc.
  • You cannot rely on sales to happen by themselves. It's up to you

» You, Inc. should always present a professional image to its prospects, customers, vendors and the public in general. Use AYB Table Stakes Marketing Toolkit
  • The "toolkit" includes templates and worksheets to help you create You, Inc.'s business cards, email address, key forms and stationery, a basic website and your elevator pitch

» Let technology help you be more productive and efficient with your limited time and give You, Inc. a competitive edge. Using your smartphone and your computer, there are easy-to-use, low cost solutions to accomplish important tasks like:
  • Finance and accounting
  • Time tracking and billing

- Job estimating
- Managing payments
- Personal organization
- General reference

# CHAPTER 12

# At Your Best: Halftime

# YOU ARE AT YOUR BEST
## *by assessing, adjusting and persisting.*

---

## AT YOUR BEST THROUGH REGULAR REVIEW

"Halftime" for You, Inc. is any time you can spend considering which aspects of the business need attention and improvement. Your long-term success depends on your ability to build on the positive and learn from and react to the negative. You need to remain flexible and objective so that you can look at all aspects of your business as they really are. Then, you have to be prepared to make the necessary mid-course corrections and refinements.

Consider adopting as an objective for yourself, the habit of always making incremental, continual improvements similar to the concept presented in *Raving Fans:* **Deliver the Vision Plus 1 Percent**. Try to regularly and consistently do your best to deliver as close to your vision of what You, Inc. could be. In those areas where You, Inc. may not yet be ready to deliver on your full vision of what it could offer, be sure to focus on those elements of your business that you know You, Inc. can deliver no matter what, and set expectations accordingly. Then, push You, Inc. to go beyond by committing to continually improving a bit at a time—a 1 percent improvement—in order to get closer and closer to your ultimate vision for You, Inc.

At minimum, you need to be able to answer and/or take action on the following questions:

- ✓ Are your current/past customers your best source to find new customers?
- ✓ What is your cash position and what are the expenses against it, now?
  - How many months of cash do you have on hand to cover you projected expenses?
- ✓ How are you doing with your expected budget versus your Sales Forecast?
- ✓ Are your "guerrilla" marketing efforts as effective as they need to be?
- ✓ Are you delivering for your "force multipliers" and are they for you?
- ✓ Are you ready to bring on a team member(s)?
- ✓ Are the processes and resources in place to hire new team members?
- ✓ Are you the type of leader that you would want to follow?
- ✓ Is your business positioned to grow, to decline or to tread water (meaning decline)?

## WHATEVER IT IS, SWOT IT

You are on your own. You launched You, Inc. and you are seeing your efforts bearing fruit. Now, is the best time to consider how things are going and if there are changes that you should make. The choices and decisions that you make on behalf of You, Inc. at this early stage can mean success or failure. However, you have made it this far because of your commitment to the principles of 3P+A as a Craftsman. You have set a strong, solid foundation for your success.

You need to constantly review how you are executing against your go-to-market planning. Where do you need to make adjustments? Where are you and You, Inc. hitting the mark and how can you capitalize on your successes? Where are you missing the mark and what changes should you be making to redirect your efforts? You need to cold-bloodedly—without wishful thinking—compare your actual results against your expectations so you can continually improve your chances of long-term success.

Remember, you have a very easy-to-use tool at your disposal anytime you are about to tackle any major issue. SWOT it early and often. Burn it into your thinking: Strengths, Weaknesses, Opportunities and Threats.

Grab a sheet of paper or a piece of plywood or whatever is close by, draw the four quadrants, and take a few minutes to be your own best coach. Ask yourself a set of better questions and you will come up with a better set of answers. Be specific the issue/decision points you want to tackle. Avoid generalities when you are fleshing out your quadrants. Whatever it is, SWOT it!

**Ask yourself:**

1. What **Strengths** does You, Inc. have to call on in taking this course of action?
2. What **Weaknesses** could impact You, Inc. when taking this course of action?
3. What **Opportunities** could open to You, Inc. by taking this course of action?
4. What **Threats** will You, Inc. have to deal with by taking this course of action?

## SUCCESS AS A LEADER OF A SMALL TEAM

Among the most important decisions you will ever make on behalf of You, Inc. will be those associates you hire to join the You, Inc. team. It is not overstating when I say that who you hire will make or break You, Inc. Your vision of what You, Inc. can become depends on selecting, leading and building the team that will work with you to meet the challenge that you have set for yourself and for You, Inc.

It starts with great hiring. Take the time to find the best. Don't accept mediocrity for the efficiency of filling a job. You will regret that many times over—not to mention the damage to your business and You, Inc.'s reputation. Think about high level skills as a Craftsman as a "must-have." Think about the soft skills (3P+A) as the tie-breaker.

At this stage in your career, you know better than most how to identify the skills and other attributes that a new hire needs to show you as you build out your team. Your objective should be to assemble and lead a team of like-minded Craftsmen, committed to the principles of 3P+A. For the purpose of being **At Your Best**, the following discussion on the You, Inc. team speaks to you as the leader of You, Inc.

There are probably more business books written about effective leadership than any other subject. I am going to suggest that there is a great book for you to read if you want to learn how to lead a small team to work together to overcome heavy odds to accomplish great things. The book was written by two former US Navy SEALs, who lay out the leadership principles embodied by every US Navy SEAL who successfully completes the extraordinarily rigorous mental and physical training. The title of the book is *Extreme Ownership: How U.S. Navy SEALs Lead and Win* by Jocko Willink and Leif Babin.

You could say that operating and leading a small business in the Skilled Trades is not the same thing as leading a small team of highly trained, highly motivated specialists focused on accomplishing a mutually agreed upon objective . . . or you could say that that is exactly what you need for your small business. You need to follow one critically important example set by the SEALs. They demand an extremely high level of skill and integrity from every individual they allow onto their team. You, Inc.'s success depends on your ability to build and lead a team of members with the positive, can-do attitude to match your own, and the skills to do the job at hand—day in and day out.

Extreme Ownership will help you see how you—as You, Inc.'s leader—can turn your team into an unstoppable force—however small or large it may turn out to be. The book and its authors present the SEAL leadership principles by first describing each principle in terms of its application in a combat or military situation followed by a business application of that principle. The principles are as clear and straightforward to understand as they are unforgiving in their demands on you as the leader. Below is a very brief summary of the principles presented in *Extreme Ownership*:

1. The leader is always responsible for every team member and every deliverable expected from each team member. This is **"Extreme Ownership"**: the leader owns all the mistakes and failures made by the team. There are no bad teams, just bad leaders.

2. The leader must be a "true believer" in the vision or else no one else on the team is going to be. The leader's belief and commitment are the first step to getting each team member to believe.

3. The leader needs to "check the ego" because it gets in the way of effective leadership. Leaders should operate with a high degree of humility ready to admit mistakes and give credit to team members.

4. The leader should recognize that working as a team results in a better outcome for everyone versus having a group of individuals doing work independently. Leaders keep their teams focused on realizing the overall vision.

5. The leader lays out what needs to be accomplished clearly and simply to avoid confusion or misunderstandings. If a team member does not understand an objective, the leader takes responsibility for not having been clear enough in presenting the vision in the appropriate terms.

6. The leader meets a challenge or difficult situation by first evaluating the highest priority problem(s) and laying out simple and clear assessments of the problem. Then the leader seeks comments or insights from the other team members. Finally, the leader uses that information to offer a clear breakdown of the process to resolve the situation. Once the first priority item is addressed, only then should the leader continue on to the next priority following the same approach, and so on.

7. The leader must act decisively, even when things around the team are uncertain and chaotic. The leader's demeanor is reflected by the team, especially in times of high stress or uncertainty. 3P+A needs to be your everyday demeanor and it needs to be what you expect of your team—day in and day out.

8. The leader must be able to lead and manage "up the chain of command." In the case of you as the leader of You, Inc.—a small business in the Skilled Trades—you need to be an effective leader, on behalf of your team, when communicating difficult-to-deal-with information to people like a general contractor or your customer, who are "up the chain of command."

9. The leader must be able to deal with the counterbalancing objectives that make up being an effective leader:

- A leader must lead but also be ready to follow
- A leader is not intimidated by a team member who knows more or is a better Craftsman
- A leader must be aggressive but not overbearing
- A leader must be calm and logical but not robotic or devoid of emotion
- A leader must be confident but humble
- A leader must be attentive to details but not obsessed by them
- A leader must be close with other team members, but not too close
- A leader has nothing to prove but everything to prove

## ✕ AYB ASSIST

*Extreme Ownership* ends each chapter with a 1–2 page section called "PRINCIPLE" and another called "Application to Business." If you are pressed for time, at least read the "PRINCIPLE" sections for chapters 1–4, 6–7, and 10–12
*The Art of the Start*—Chap. 6 "The Art of Recruiting"

## YOU, INC. & YOUR EMPLOYEES AND CONTRACTORS

With its first employee other than yourself, You, Inc. becomes a different animal in terms of the paperwork that you need to track and file. Whether you are dealing with independent contractors or actual employees of You, Inc., you must do the right things at the right time or else deal with some potentially difficult ramifications from local, state and federal government agencies.

Suffice it to say that you simply do not want to ignore or take short-cuts concerning the requirements imposed by these agencies. These requirements will be different by state and possibly by city so do your homework.

## AYB ASSIST

*Small Time Operator*—Chap. 3 "Growing Up"—read at least the first ten pages

---

*What is important is seldom urgent and what is urgent is seldom important.*

—DWIGHT D. EISENHOWER

---

## NEVER ENOUGH TIME IN THE DAY

As a small business owner, time is not your friend. There will never be enough time to do everything that needs to be done. Still, your ability to execute on your most critical tasks—day in and day out—will largely determine You, Inc.'s success.

Everyone deals with time constraints differently and there are countless books and tools that you can look to for help. Unless you have your own approach to planning out your days to avoid feeling overwhelmed with never having enough time, my suggestion is to consider the following straightforward approach to break down how you allocate your time.

This approach is called the Eisenhower Decision Matrix because it was used by our 34th President of the United States—Dwight D. Eisenhower. This matrix allows you to break down and separate your tasks into those that are most important and urgent versus those that are less important and significant. The objective is to make sure that you have an easy-to-use, ready way to identify what you should always be focused on throughout the day.

To create your own Eisenhower Decision Matrix, do the following:

✓ Take a sheet of paper and draw a matrix that consists of four quadrants with the following labels: "Important/Urgent," "Important/Not Urgent," "Not Important/Urgent," "Not Important/Not Urgent."

✓ Fill in the matrix placing all of the tasks that you have on your always growing to-do list according to the appropriate quadrant label.

| QUADRANT 1: IMPORTANT/URGENT | QUADRANT 2: IMPORTANT/NOT URGENT |
|---|---|
| ✓ Customer deadlines and follow up calls<br>✓ Crisis—business or personal<br>✓ Tax deadline | ✓ Force multiplier networking meetings<br>✓ Next quarter business planning<br>✓ New business follow-up calls |
| QUADRANT 3: NOT IMPORTANT/URGENT | QUADRANT 4: NOT IMPORTANT/NOT URGENT |
| ✓ Interruptions<br>✓ Impromptu meetings<br>✓ Nonessential calls | ✓ Cleaning out email or bulk mail files<br>✓ Endless time wasters |

**A word about Quadrant 1 items:** There will always be uncontrollable events or situations that cannot be anticipated that will need to be dealt with irrespective of your other high priorities. However, in all honesty, most emergencies and urgent matters in business can typically be traced back to an unmet commitment or something that was left undone or that could have been done well before a deadline. Just don't let things get there.

With that said, on a daily basis try to do the following:

- ✓ Work to keep the number of Quadrant 1 activities to a minimum
- ✓ Take every opportunity to spend more time on Quadrant 2 activities. Take the time to think through activities before having to do so when you are up against the wall with urgent issues.
- ✓ Cut your time spent on Quadrant 3 and 4 activities whenever possible
- ✓ Force yourself to stay focused on things that make a difference, even if it is hard to do

Once you get comfortable with doing this exercise on your own, you might consider doing the exercise with your team. In that way, if you and your team are experiencing any issues with time constraints and setting priorities, as a team, you could use the Eisenhower Decision Matrix to get everyone on the same page.

## Saying "No" Sometimes Is the Right Answer

One of the surest ways that you have to put some limits on your runaway to-do list is to simply say "No" to Quadrant 3 and 4 items before they even get on your list in the first place. If something is "Not Important," is there really any good reason to waste any time worrying about it?

Another critically important consideration when deciding whether to say "Yes" or "No" is on decisions related to new business. It is always worse in terms of reputation, costs and customer service to accept an additional job when You, Inc. is not able to deliver a high-quality work product from start to finish. Sometimes saying "No" to new business is the right answer.

## Plan Your Day the Night Before and Sleep Better

Surely, it is not news to you that one of the main causes for insomnia or lack of sleep is worrying about forgetting something or thinking about what you have to do the next day. Attack this problem head-on and sleep better at night.

Take some time at the end of the day to list out what you need to accomplish the next day—if you can do it on an Eisenhower Decision Matrix all the better. Then, let your subconscious mind work on the problems while you sleep. You might surprise yourself at the solutions you might come with in the morning. Better still, when you wake up, you will know exactly what needs to be done as you start your day.

**AYB Quick Tool:** Go to www.AtYourBest.com and click on "**AYB Quick Tools**" for a simple, Microsoft Excel–based **Eisenhower Decision Matrix** worksheet that you can download and easily modify for your purposes.

## IMPROVE OR REMOVE

You, Inc. does not have the luxury of repeating mistakes or putting up with substandard elements of your business. Take the opportunity during these Halftime reassessment sessions to consider what is working and what isn't. For those parts or players in your business that are not working toward the intended objective, take a cold, clear-eyed look at the issue at hand and then IMPROVE or REMOVE.

Wishful thinking or hoping for outcomes that cannot or will not come true is not something You, Inc. can afford right now—or ever really. There is never a good reason to let a subpar aspect of your business fester or get worse. The sooner you address it head-on—fix it or make a change—the better for You, Inc. and for everyone involved.

Get in the habit of regularly reviewing, making adjustments and rethinking the follow questions:

- ✓ Is You, Inc.'s Go-to-Marketing Plan hitting the mark?
- ✓ How are You, Inc.'s financials tracking?
- ✓ How is the You, Inc. team shaping up?

### Is Your Go-to-Market Plan Hitting the Mark?

At least on a monthly basis, take some time to do a Halftime review of You, Inc.'s Go-to-Market Plan. Even if you only do so in your head, make sure you are going through how you are doing against your expected results. Identify those elements of your plan that need attention or were completely off the mark. Ask a better question and you will get a better answer.

### How are You, Inc.'s Financials Tracking?

At least weekly, spend time reviewing You, Inc.'s financial position and the parts of your business affecting cashflow. How is your cashflow tracking compared to projected, upcoming outflows? How are your business development efforts to identify new, prospective customers working as compared to your pipeline of future business? What is reality and what may be wishing thinking? What are you going to do about it?

## *How is the You, Inc. Team Shaping Up?*

At least on a daily basis, think about how your team is delivering on your vision of what You, Inc. can be. Are they adopting You, Inc.'s version of a 3P+A mindset to turn your customers into "Raving Fans?" Are you as the leader of You, Inc. "walking the walk" of taking "Extreme Ownership" with your team? If not on one or the other or both, what are you planning on doing to improve your results? Have the hard conversations early and directly to help your team members improve and for everyone to stay on track.

## GET BACK ON THE FIELD

Halftime is over. Get back on the field. Avoid paralysis by analysis. You, Inc. needs your head in the game. Your customer needs you to deliver on the expectations that You, Inc. set for them. Your team needs their leader leading. Analysis does not pay the bills. Execution and continual improvement does.

## —————— CHAPTER 12 REPLAY ——————
## At Your Best: Halftime

» You, Inc.'s long-term success depends on your ability to regularly build on the positives and learn from the negatives—remaining flexible and objective and seeing things as the really are. Ask yourself:
  • How is You, Inc. doing against its Go-To-Market Plan?
  • How is You, Inc. tracking with its financials?
  • How is the You, Inc. team shaping up?
  • Where do you need to improve or make a change?

» Whatever it is, SWOT it

- Draw the four quadrants and lay out the elements of your decision or issue
- Ask yourself better questions so you can find better answers

» Leading a small team to accomplish great things against more established competitors and other market forces requires "extreme ownership" on your part as a leader

» There will never be enough time in the day to do everything that you might want to do

- Use the Eisenhower Decision Matrix to prioritize your limited time on the most important tasks first, while separating out time-consuming or unproductive activities

# Getting Your Head Straight, Part 2

# Getting Your Head Straight, Part 2

# YOU ARE AT YOUR BEST
## *when you can keep your head straight, even in trying times.*

---

## GETTING YOUR HEAD STRAIGHT, PART 2

Now is the time to offer up a few more "attitude adjusters" that are oriented more to the challenges that You, Inc. will encounter as a small business.

Businesses of all sizes, just like professional athletes, look to business coaches, trainers and mentors to help them be at their best. However, You, Inc. doesn't have a budget for a business coach or trainer to help guide you and your team to meet business objectives and overcome challenges and obstacles. For better or worse, it is up to you to "get your head straight" when self-doubt and second-guessing your life choices creep into your thinking.

As in "Getting Your Head Straight, Part 1," the following lays out some "SME Insights" and "Quotes to Get Your Head Straight" divided among the 3P+A categories. Also, there are additional motivational quotes as well as some thoughts offered by AYB Subject Matter Experts (SME) offered on the **At Your Best** website.

**AYB Quick Tool:** Go to www.AtYourBest.com and click on "**AYB Quick Tools**." You will find a link to **Getting Your Head Straight**. All the quotes are grouped according to their focus and then categorized under one of four headings: People, Performance, Professionalism and Attitude, or 3P+A. The comments provided by the SMEs are presented under those categories as "SME Insights."

Now, as in Chapter 8, read through the following insights and quotes and take a moment to pick the two in each group that resonate with you or impact you when you first read them. Then, put a check mark in the space next to it. Your objective is to find a couple attitude adjusters in each of the 3P+A categories that you can quickly refer back to when things get hectic and challenging.

## PEOPLE: THE FIRST P IN 3P+A

### SME Insights about People:

*A big mistake new business owners make: they buy a big, flashy truck with a sign on the side to show how successful they are. Then, they end up working for that truck instead of their client or their long-term business success.*

—JEFF M., CONTRACTOR, ST. LOUIS

*Your reputation opens doors, but you still have to sell yourself and your team on every job—no matter how big or small your business might be.*

—GEORGE M., CONTRACTOR, NEW YORK

*When you buy a piece of equipment for the company, assign it to one person. Then, you know it will be taken care of and who to look to if it breaks down.*

—DAVE M., CONTRACTOR, SEATTLE AREA

## Quotes to Get Your Head Straight about People:

*The more you engage with customers the clearer things become and the easier it is to determine what you should be doing.*

—JOHN RUSSELL

*You need to spend all your time and energy on creating something that actually brings value to the people you're asking for money.*

—GARY VAYNERCHUK

*It takes years to build a reputation and five minutes to ruin it. If you think about that, you'll do things differently.*

—WARREN BUFFETT

*Every contact we have with a customer influences whether or not they'll come back. We have to be great every time or we will lose them.*

—KEVIN STIRTZ

*Rule #1—If we don't take care of the customer . . . somebody else will.*

—EDGAR MITCHELL

*Everyone is not your customer.*

—SETH GODIN

*Don't try to tell the customer what he wants. If you want to be smart, be smart in the shower. Then get out, go to work and serve the customer.*

—GENE BUCKLEY

*Loyal customers, they don't just come back, they don't simply recommend you, they insist that their friends do business with you.*

—CHIP BELL

*Every great business is built on friendship.*

—JC PENNEY

## PERFORMANCE: THE SECOND P IN 3P+A

### SME Insights about Performance:

*Plan to be the wearer of many hats and learn to wear each one of them as if it was made especially for you.*

—GARY C., CONTRACTOR, SEATTLE AREA

*You can't use your back to make it as a contractor. You have to use your head. Your back will only get you so far before it gives out or just gets old.*

—AL B., CONTRACTOR, NEW YORK

*The harder you work, the more work you get. The more work you get, the more customers you take from your competition. The moral of the story: The harder you work, the better it is for you and the worse it is for your competition. Any questions?*

—MARIO M., CONTRACTOR, NEW YORK

### Quotes to Get Your Head Straight about Performance:

*In the world of business, the people who are most successful are those who are doing what they love.*

—WARREN BUFFETT

*Once you agree upon the price you and your family must pay for success, it enables you to ignore the minor hurts, the opponent's pressure and the temporary failures.*

—VINCE LOMBARDI

*Success doesn't come to you, you go to it.*

—MARVA COLLINS

*The only place where success comes before work is in the dictionary.*

—VINCE LOMBARDI

*Anything worth doing hurts a little.*

—MIKE ROWE

*Everything negative—pressure, challenges—are all an opportunity for me to rise.*

—KOBE BRYANT

*When everything seems to be going against you, remember that the airplane takes off against the wind, not with it.*

—HENRY FORD

*Attack each day with an enthusiasm unknown to mankind.*

—JIM HARBAUGH

*Today is another chance, make yourself proud.*

—UNKNOWN

*Your work is going to fill a large part of your life, and the only way to be truly satisfied is to do what you believe is great work. And the only way to do great work is to love what you do.*

—STEVE JOBS

## PROFESSIONALISM: THE THIRD P IN 3P+A

### *SME Insights about Professionalism:*

*Do your best work when no one is watching you and your work will be covered by sheetrock.*

—RUSS M., CONTRACTOR, SEATTLE AREA

*Customers don't expect you to be perfect every time. They do expect that you will make it right. You have to be prepared to tell them the bad news before they figure it out some other way and you have to tell how you are going to make it right.*

—RICHARD S., CONTRACTOR, NEW YORK

*Every day, every job, every invoice is another chance to build on or ruin your reputation. Make it a habit to always tell yourself: 'Doing the right thing is ALWAYS the right thing.'*

—CALVIN M., CONTRACTOR, SEATTLE AREA

## Quotes to Get Your Head Straight about Professionalism:

*You have to perform at a consistently higher level than others. That's is the mark of a true professional.*

—JOE PATERNO

*Hold yourself responsible for a higher standard than anyone else expects of you. Never excuse yourself.*

—HENRY FORD

*Our true character is that person we become when no one is watching.*

—JOHN WOODEN

*If plan A fails, remember there are 25 more letters.*

—CLAIRE COOK

*The price of success is hard work, dedication to the job at hand and the determination that whether we win or lose, we have applied the best of ourselves to the task at hand.*

—VINCE LOMBARDI

*He that is good for making excuses is seldom good for anything else.*

—BENJAMIN FRANKLIN

*You can't have a million-dollar dream with a minimum wage work ethic.*

—STEPHEN C. HOGAN

*Either you run the day, or the day runs you.*

—JIM ROHN

*There is no passion to be found playing small—settling for a life that is less than the one you are capable of living.*

—NELSON MANDELA

*You can't build a reputation on what you are going to do.*

—HENRY FORD

## ATTITUDE: THE A IN 3P+A

### SME Insights about Attitude:

---

*As a small businessperson, you are living the American Dream in the greatest country in the world. Smile and get on with it. There is nothing that will come your way that a positive attitude cannot make better. On the other hand, there is anything that can happen—good or bad—that will be madworse with a bad attitude. It is always your choice.*

— ALBERTO F., CONTRACTOR, NEW YORK

*There is no place on my team for someone with a negative, pessimistic attitude, who complains and whines all the time—and that includes me.*

— BRYAN A., CONTRACTOR, SEATTLE AREA

*When the going gets tough, take a minute to let it sink in and to look for a solution. Then, get your butt in gear and make something good happen.*

— JEFF C., CONTRACTOR, SEATTLE AREA

---

## Quotes to Get Your Head Straight about Attitude:

*Whether you think that you can or think that you can't—you're right.*

—HENRY FORD

*A pessimist sees the difficulty in every opportunity; an optimist sees the opportunity in every difficulty.*

—WINSTON CHURCHILL

*Nothing of any importance has ever been accomplished by a pessimist.*

—JACK WELCH

*Make sure that your worst enemy doesn't live between your own two ears.*

—LAIRD HAMILTON

*If you get up in the morning expecting to have a bad day, you rarely disappoint yourself.*

—WAYNE DYER

*Attitudes are contagious. Make yours worth catching.*

—MARY KAY

*I am the greatest, I said that even before I knew I was.*

—MUHAMMAD ALI

*Optimism is the most important human trait, because it allows us to evolve our ideas, to improve our situation and to hope for a better tomorrow.*

—SETH GODIN

*It's hard to beat a person who never gives up.*

—BABE RUTH

*Small business isn't for the faint of heart. It's for the brave, the patient and the persistent. It's for the overcomers.*

—UNKNOWN

## CHAPTER 13 REPLAY
### Getting Your Head Straight, Part 2

» As the saying goes: "It's lonely at the top." You are at the top of You, Inc. and there will be many times when you will need to "get your head back in the game."

  • Replace self-doubt and negativity with new empowering, positive thoughts

» When necessary, do the following:
- Read through the insights and quotes
- Select the two in each group that resonate with you
- Write them down and post them where you can see them often
- Then, hitch up your pants and get back to work

» Only you can control your attitude—all day, every day

# CHAPTER 14

# At Your Best: Going Pro

# YOU ARE AT YOUR BEST
## *as you grow You, Inc.*

### AT YOUR BEST GOING TO THE "NEXT LEVEL"

You have built one heck of a business! Your small business is thriving, and you are now thinking about what it will take to play on a much larger field. Admittedly, many of the concepts that you have adopted to be **At Your Best** as well as those that you have used to build your small business will serve you well in your future endeavors.

Your success has now gotten you to the point where there can be no doubt in anyone's mind that you know what you are doing and that you know how to run a thriving business. However, just like all world-class athletes need their coaches and trainers to be at their best, you now need your group of "assistant coaches and trainers". (For instance: accountant, attorney, bookkeeper, office manager, job site supervisor(s) and managers, etc.) to help you and You, Inc. to continue be **At Your Best**.

This is the last of the Kitchen Table Moments that I will be pointing out for you in this AYB Playbook. Your answers to the questions below will confirm that it is time to build out your team of coaches and trainers. With every "YES" answer, the greater the requirement will be that you need to act sooner than later. Take note of how you answer the following questions:

✓ Have you become a bottleneck? Are you slowing your firm's growth potential?

✓ Are you turning down jobs because your team is spread too thinly?

✓ Do you have predictable, reliable sources of revenue?

✓ Do you need outside financing in order to grow to the next level?

✓ Do you need new or more large equipment to go to the next level?

✓ Do you need to bring on an additional, new team with a manager?

✓ Do you want to attack new opportunities outside your local market?

✓ Do you want to expand your service offering beyond your core set?

✓ Are you ready to take on more? More risk for more potential reward?

✓ One last time, whatever "it" is . . . Is it realistic? Did you SWOT it?

If your answers are predominantly "YES" to these questions, then it is time for you to expand your horizons. You have done well in realizing your American Dream by being **At Your Best** as you built your career as an HVAC/R Technician and then you built a thriving small business. Now, it is time to create the next chapter of the You, Inc. Playbook by surrounding yourself with other seasoned professionals that can help you leverage your reach and effectiveness. I am confident that great things are in store for You, Inc.

## ───────── CHAPTER 14 REPLAY ─────────
## At Your Best: Going Pro

» Congratulations! You followed the game plan laid out in this AYB Playbook and You, Inc. is a success.

» To keep You, Inc. thriving, you need to build out your management team by asking yourself: Who are those key additional people that I can bring on to help You, Inc. to:

- Grow the team to expand You, Inc. business without compromising quality?
- Build and grow the foundation of predictable sources of revenue?
- Secure additional funding to underwrite the expansion of You, Inc.?

» Always be **At Your Best**

# GLOSSARY OF TERMS

## www.AtYourBest.com

www.AtYourBest.com—The **At Your Best** website and the AYB Playbooks are designed to work together to give you access to the broadest set of resources you will need as you build your career and business in the Skilled Trades. The AYB Playbooks are intentionally kept concise to make them easy to read and kept close by for easy, quick reference. The www.AtYourBest.com site is designed to include many additional resources and tools to help you be successful.

## 3P+A

3P+A stands for **People, Performance, Professionalism & Attitude**. It is a fundamental concept of **At Your Best** intended to be a simple way to always remember your success in the Skilled Trades and as a small business comes down to: how you work with People on the job; how you Perform on the job; how Professional you are whenever you are on the job; and critically important, how you control your Attitude on the job.

## AYB Assist

**AYB Assist** is a quick way to find additional information concerning a topic discussed in this AYB Playbook. The **AYB Assist** directs you to specific sections or chapters in the books recommended in this AYB Playbook to quickly learn more about a subject without having to read the entire book.

## AYB Quick Tool

**AYB Quick Tool** refers to an inventory of tools developed along with this AYB Playbook to help you accomplish a wide array of tasks discussed in the Playbook. You can access this ever-growing set of tools by going to www.AtYourBest.com and clicking on **"AYB Quick Tools"** where you will find links to all the tools.

## AYB Playbook

AYB Playbook is intended to be your game plan for success in the Skilled Trades, giving you the minimum set of "plays" you need to execute to be successful as a Craftsman and a small business.

## Craftsman

Craftsman is the term used to help you be **At Your Best** and differentiate yourself by always focusing on improving your skills so that your attitude and work product are always of the highest level.

## Elevator Pitch

Elevator Pitch is a brief (20–30 second) persuasive set of talking points that you can use to spark the interest of your listener(s). You use an elevator pitch to present your unique value proposition in an easy, comfortable manner, which takes a lot of practice to accomplish well. You need to have your practiced elevator pitches ready whether you are looking for a job as an employee speaking with a prospective boss or as the VP of Sales and Business Development speaking with a prospective client or force multiplier.

## Force Multiplier

Force multiplier is any person or business whose position gives them access to jobs, customers and prospects that you would love to have as your own. You build your "team" of force multipliers by focusing on trying to answer the following question: What is in it for them?

## Guerrilla Marketing and Other "Guerrilla" Business Strategies

Guerrilla marketing and other "guerrilla" business concepts are strategies designed for small businesses with few resources and limited budgets to aggressively promote their products or services in unconventional ways. To be successful, guerrilla campaigns businesspeople leverage their high energy, innovation, imagination and time to capture the attention and loyalty of the public on a more personal and memorable level. "Guerrilla Marketing" was coined by Jay Conrad Levinson.

## Kitchen Table Moment

Kitchen Table Moment refers to those times when you may be sitting at your kitchen table, alone or with someone important to you, trying to think through decisions of what the right steps are to take to ensure that you will be successful. This AYB Playbook offers a great deal of questions presented at each stage of your career path that you can consider during those Kitchen Table Moments.

## Subject Matter Expert (SME)

Subject Matter Expert refers to one of the skilled Craftsmen or small business people who offered their insights in developing the **At Your Best** Playbook series and the www.AtYourBest.com website. SMEs have "been there, done that" and were all more than willing to help make the content provided as useful and pertinent as possible.

## SWOT Analysis

SWOT stands for **Strengths, Weaknesses, Opportunities** and **Threats**. A SWOT analysis is an exercise that allows you to assess your business decisions by listing the specific elements of the decisions in terms of their strengths and weaknesses (internal) and opportunities and threats (external) in an easy-to-use four-quadrant matrix.

## You, Inc.

You, Inc. is one of the key, core concepts of **At Your Best**. You, Inc. refers to you as both a skilled Craftsman when you are an employee and when you are launching your small business.

- ✓ You, Inc. has services to sell: Your skills, experience and work product
- ✓ You, Inc.'s clients pay you for your services: Your employer or your customer
- ✓ You, Inc.'s success is built on execution: Your reputation for quality

# LIST OF AYB QUICK TOOLS

You can access all the **AYB Quick Tools** listed in this AYB Playbook as listed below as well as many others that will be created over time, as you and our other readers make their suggestions and requests. Go to www .AtYourBest.com and click on "**AYB Quick Tools.**"

| AYB QUICK TOOL | PURPOSE OF AYB QUICK TOOL |
|---|---|
| Client How-to-do Ratings | Instructions for your clients for Angie's List and HomeAdvisor |
| Eisenhower Decision Matrix | Worksheet and examples to help manage your time for You, Inc. |
| Elevator Pitch | Worksheet and example(s) to develop your elevator pitches |
| Expense Budget | Worksheet and example(s) to enter your initial Expense Budget |
| Find Certifications | Instructions to find certification programs for Skilled Trades |
| Find Local Apprenticeship | Instructions to find local apprenticeship program |
| Find Local Financial Aid | Instructions to find local sources of financial aid for your education |
| Find Local Training | Instructions to find local vocational training |
| Find Resources for Veterans | Instructions to find local resources for veterans |
| Getting Your Head Straight | Great motivational quotes listed by category to read and adjust your attitude |

| Job Search Action Plan | Worksheet and example to build your plan to launch your job search |
|---|---|
| Licensing Information Websites | List of agency websites by State specifying licensing requirements |
| Profit & Loss Statement | Worksheet and example(s) to create your initial P&L |
| Quick Win Brainstorming | Worksheet and example(s) to brainstorm your quick wins |
| Resumes for the Skilled Trades | Sample resumes and guidance to create your own resume |
| Salary Finder | Instructions to find local salary range in Skilled Trade |
| Sales Forecast | Worksheet and example(s) to enter your initial Sales Forecast |
| SME Interview Highlights | Key points made by Subject Matter Experts during interviews |
| Startup Expenses | Worksheet and example(s) to enter your initial startup costs |
| SWOT Analysis | Worksheet and example(s) to use for a SWOT analysis |
| Table Stakes Marketing Toolkit | Group of **AYB Quick Tools** included in single folder for easy access |
| Timing & Action Plan | Worksheet and example(s) to plan out your timing and actions |
| You, Inc. Business Card | Microsoft Word template for easy printing of business cards |
| You, Inc. Business Email Address | Instructions to set up a business email address with Gmail |
| You, Inc. Business Mailing Address | Instructions to set up a PO Box with USPS & UPS Store |
| You, Inc. Forms & Stationery | Easy-to-use Microsoft Word–based templates for You, Inc. correspondence |
| You, Inc. Business Website | Instructions to create a professional website without being technical |

# AFTERWORD

I want to thank you for reading this AYB Playbook. I sincerely hope that what you read here will help you be **At Your Best** in your quest to realize your American Dream. I truly look forward to hearing about all your successes.

I will consider it an honor and a true measure of success for **At Your Best**, if you find that you end up using this AYB Playbook and our website as an ongoing reference as you build your successful career and your small business. Let me know how it goes. If along the way, you find that this AYB Playbook or the www.AtYourBest.com website can be improved in any way, please send me an email at Comments2JC@AtYourBest.com. I promise that I will act on your suggestion.

Well, I guess this really is it. I wish you all the best.

Juan Carosso
Kingston, Washington